PRAISE FOR *SAFETY NETWORK*

"*SAFETY NETwork*, should be required reading in every MBA program. Vitally important to any successful executive are the skills and processes needed to create a thriving community of connections. You'll find them inside the pages of *SAFETY NETwork*!"
Hank O'Donnell, CPCC; Master Chair, Vistage International

"Garber has artfully captured the experiences, feelings, and challenges so many senior executives face in our changing economy and world of work and has reminded us that each person we meet may well have an unexpected story that gives us a new lens through which to see our own."
Diane James, Executive Director, Greater Philadelphia Senior Executive Group (GPSEG)

"Garber understands well the need for and the best way to build a truly supportive network. This book shows how it can be done."
Richard Guha, Chairman, International Executive Resource Group (IERG)

"With *SAFETY NETwork*, Garber has mastered the art of allegorical storytelling. She wove a story that I couldn't put down and at the same time created a very practical checklist that all executives should follow, no matter how secure you feel in your current position. The bottom line is that coaching and networking are invaluable career tools and shouldn't just be part of an outplacement process."
Chicke Fitzgerald, Founder, Executive Girlfriends Group (EGG)

"Garber has written a terrific story about the trials and tribulations of executives in various stages of career transition. *SAFETY NETwork* is a must read for anyone who still has a long career ramp to help prepare them for the inevitable bumps in the road that we will all face."
Joe Tait, Chapter President, Society For Information Management (SIM)

"*SAFETY NETwork* illustrates the importance of executive networking through a captivating and emotional journey."
Ann Robson, EVP & Chief Client Officer, Kelleher Associates

"There are three kinds of networking: 1. Connecting with old friends, 2. Making new friends, and 3. Introducing friends to each other. If you do all three, you can't lose."
Matt Bud, Chairman, The Financial Executives Networking Group (The FENG)

"Without executive networking, Garber's characters find themselves in a scarier place than any Stephen King story!"
Joey Iazzetto, Chairman, Marketing Executives Networking Group (MENG)

SAFETY NETwork

Suzanne Garber

SAFETY NETwork

A Tale of Ten Truths of Executive Networking

Suzanne Garber

Front Cover Image: Amanda Wuest

Printed in the United States of America

ISBN-10: 1505783585
ISBN-13: 978-1505783582

DEDICATION

For T. and the tens of thousands of executives who have lost a job and triumphed because of it. The courage, perseverance, and tenacity you exhibit are an inspiration to many and keep the economy moving forward.

Suzanne Garber

CONTENTS

Suzanne Garber

ACKNOWLEDGMENTS

Deep thanks go to the 100+ executives who voluntarily gave of their time, talent, wisdom, and network to provide the content to shape each character and resource in the Appendices. Of those able to receive public acknowledgement, this list includes: Dave Berry, Mitch Blackburn, Neil Brandmaier, Paul Bailo, Craig Bell, Rich Buchanan, Javier Daly, Andre David, Jennifer Dawn, Frank DeLuca, Bill Fallon, Monty Ferguson, Allison Hart, Jay Hemmady, Greg Holden, Jim Lee, Noel Leeson, Alan Mansfield, Roberta Matuson, Mindy Mazer, Ford Myers, Deborah Overdeput, Rob Pilgrim, Henry Pruitt, Eric Rosenbluth, Robert Rosend, Jim Rutt, Scott Salantrie, Kevin Smith, Paul Sniffin, Jeff Stollman, Joe Tait, and Blaine Taylor.

Support and communication from many of the executive networking, coaching and outplacement firms listed in the appendices also provided a solid sounding board for the need for a book like this that validates the experiences, emotions, and journeys of so many displaced executives—past, current, and future. Continue the great work you are doing in so many people's lives.

I am proud to serve the American Red Cross and salute the hundreds of thousands of volunteers and employees who give tirelessly of themselves in order to alleviate suffering by others. Thank you for your contributions to this book and our communities.

Finally, I could not do anything without my partner in life and work, Christopher Garber, who gives me freedom, acceptance, and unconditional love.

INTRODUCTION

"Hello?" The still, small voice on the other end of the phone was unintelligible and foreign to me.

"Hi, it's Suz. Merry Christmas!"

The response was not nearly as enthusiastic, alive or festive for either the season or my memory of who this person was. This person was a respected colleague, trusted friend, and accomplished professional who had gone from having everything to absolutely nothing over the course of twenty-four months.

My friend transitioned from living in an opulent downtown townhome with a trendy sports car in a mid-western city in a senior management position with a Fortune 500 firm to living in a shelter who now owned a total of 5 suitcases filled with clothes, books, and other personal items to her name. After having been a part of a massive restructuring and downsizing effort at the company two years prior, a spate of bad luck and sometimes-uninformed decisions had led to the current situation.

I sent my friend a one-way train ticket to come live with my family during the process of picking up the pieces of life. It was hoped that, by having a stable environment in which to live, network and regain self-confidence that this person would be back on the road to professional recovery and success—to the extent and level that this person was accustomed to and could be once again.

After six months of processing the pain, anger, and hurt, and then moving forward in a positive manner of networking, making meaningful professional acquaintances, and truly understanding one's skill set, this person is now back amongst the professionally viable, vibrant and verifiable. However, it did not come without its pain, struggles, and frustrations.

Spurred on by the initial lack of traction and success my friend was finding, I took up the role of understanding exactly how does executive networking work and how do terminated, laid off or downsized executives maintain success, resiliency, and confidence in the wake of an ongoing unstable economic outlook—particularly if they have not taken care to build their own safety network throughout their career ascension. Thus, I sent out a query to my vast professional network of executives around the world to ask if any had stories of triumph and overcoming adversity as it related to losing one's job that they would like to share. I was flooded with responses from CEOs, COOs, CIOs, CFOs, VPs, Directors and other executives who wanted to share their stories, tips, and anecdotes to this project.

Ironically, my company chose to acknowledge my abilities at connecting people, organizations, and services around the globe by appointing me "Chief Networking Officer." Responsible for overseeing the relationships and teams who provide service to the tens of millions of international expatriates, students, and travelers around the globe, I aligned needs with services and people with products. Ultimately, my position, too, was eliminated and I utilized the tactics and strategies outlined here to land smoothly on my own safety net.

In short, no one is safe. But, everyone can be prepared.

SAFETY NETwork is the compilation of over one hundred confidential interviews with mostly C-level executives who have experienced the humiliation, defeat, and setback due to termination, layoff and downsizing yet overcome it to now be at peace with wherever they are in life. Many have resumed or even surpassed previous positions. Some have made complete changes in their professional goals. Many went back to school. Some took their for-profit experience to now lead non-profit organizations. Whatever the term used for reduction in workforce—whether on a grand scale or an individual one—each executive has a story to tell of lessons learned, objectives achieved, and adversity overcome.

This book is not for everyone. This book is geared almost exclusively for executives of a certain income level and title. If you are not already at this level, it will not help you get a promotion into the executive halls although it may help you understand the dynamics, benefits, and pitfalls of a career at this level. If you are already at this level, the lessons ascribed here will help you maintain your emotional stability, professional composure, and personal resiliency, confidence, and self worth in the midst of seemingly overwhelming defeat.

Take heart and realize you are more than your title. You do have valuable contributions to make to an organization. You must avoid negativity. Find your passion(s). And, you will see that good does come from all of this. Trust me. Trust the hundreds of thousands of executives who have already learned this the hard way and overcome.

Matt Bud, Chairman of the 40,000+ member Financial Executives Networking Group (FENG) wrote me as I was putting the finishing touches on the book:

> "The French philosopher René Descartes said: I think, therefore I am. If he were alive today, he would add: I am, therefore I network. Networking creates meaningful business contacts and relationships that further your career and enhance your professional life."

Now, go develop your own safety network.

Suzanne Garber

Chapter One

The Fire

The smell wafted up his nostrils and attacked his sinuses. Smoke clogged his airways as he began to choke. Halfway dazed from the 2/3 bottle of Fonseca Port he had drunk a few hours earlier which caused him to fall asleep on his couch, he realized he needed to do something quickly. First, of which, was to wake up and fully assess the situation.

Damn, he thought as flames started dancing around him and catching other pieces of the carpet. "I have to get up and get out of here". His legs didn't want to cooperate and his attempts at hoisting his 230 pound frame off of the Ligne Roset leather sofa were going unheeded. He may be drunk but he was lucid enough to know he was in trouble if he didn't either put the fire out or get out of there quickly.

He flung himself onto the floor, almost directly into the heat of the quickly igniting blaze. He made a few small attempts to smack the fire out but it was now well beyond what his unprotected hands could smother. Plus, he was still wearing his charcoal herringbone Hickey Freeman suit that he had worn to work only 4 hours earlier. Not like he might be wearing it again, but he still didn't want to ruin a perfectly tailored suit. He'd already torn off his Italian silk tie after leaving the PhasInt building and tossed it on the floor upon arrival to his apartment. He now watched it consumed in the flames.

He lurched forward for a few moments before having his neurons connect panic from his brain to pain in his hand. Floundering on the floor trying to both get away from and pound out the sparks and flames on the carpet for what seemed an eternity, the fire danced eerily around him. The combustion had reached the pile of papers and reports he had brought home from work a few days prior in preparation of an upcoming meeting on Monday. Up they went in an instant, like the kindling he would stack as a Boy Scout ready to roast marshmallows at the campfire. He had to lift his body up but his balance was unsure and wobbly. His lime green throw area rug was now completely engulfed in a contained yet precarious glow of orange. He still couldn't manage to heave himself up off the ground and thought of the irony this would be to the end of not only a bad day but also a terrible year in his life.

As fate would have it, the fire alarm went off in a loud wail. Immediately, the sprinkler system within his apartment was activated as the smoke curled upwards into the air ducts. Cool droplets of water splashed on his forehead and the surrounding area thus beginning the gradual elimination of the inferno.

His door burst open and incoming poured the building manager and several of his neighbors who had heard the fire alarm. The building manager, a buxom blonde, was carrying a portable fire extinguisher which she adeptly started spraying upon her entrance to the apartment.

"What happened in here?" she yelled, emitting white foam across the rugs, bookcase, coffee table, sofa, and his legs. Two of his neighbors, whom he had not yet met, ran over to him, each flanking him on either side.

"Are you okay?" asked a matronly looking woman in her sixties. He believed she lived next door as he had only seen her a few times leaving her apartment to pick up the mail downstairs. She patted his hand. "I should get you a glass of water. That was a close call." She quickly stood up and walked over to the kitchen. He heard her grab a glass out of the cupboard and begin filling it from the faucet. He was too dazed to tell her he didn't drink unfiltered city tap water; that's why he had installed a Kinetico K5 water filter right alongside the tap. Could he still be pretentious in the midst of near destruction?

The other, a young man in his twenties, looked at him and the smoldering carpet. To himself, the neighbor uttered, "Holy crap. That was close." He did not come closer to him and quietly edged back toward the door, preferring to be an onlooker as opposed to an active participant in the unfurling chaos.

His building manager approached him, stood directly over top of him and repeated "What the hell happened in here?" She glanced at his 2/3 empty bottle and stooped down to look at him face to face. It was not a kind look, not like the lady next door.

He couldn't speak; he felt embarrassed and ashamed. His clothes were rumpled, he was still lying on the floor and certain he smelled like alcohol and smoke. Ironically, the opened bottle of port and his empty glass were fully intact on top of the coffee table; the files of papers and reports he brought home on Thursday in preparation for a meeting on Monday had all been engulfed in the flames as they flanked the coffee table and sofa. He was fortunate he hadn't yet populated his built-in bookcase with anything other than more reports from work. They remained unscathed but would have next gone up in flames had the sprinkler system not been activated.

"Get up. We need to get you checked out. The fire department will be here any second." The building manager went to grab him by his right arm just as his neighbor brought over the glass of water.

"Do you think we should let him stay here? I mean, until the paramedics arrive?" His neighbor seemed genuinely concerned.

"No. He's got some explaining to do and I don't see that he's been hurt. Come on Mr. Pibbs. Let's get you up off the floor and over to the dining room chairs where it's not so smoky." His building manager tried to hoist him up but she was no match for his bulk. He took the glass of water from his neighbor, muttered a "thank you," and was able to sit upright for the first time since he fell asleep.

"I'm not sure what happened. I fell asleep," was all he managed to say. He gulped the water down. He couldn't look either lady in the eye. He noticed the younger man still peering at him from the front door to his apartment. He left for a second and returned with two firemen in full uniform plus a paramedic.

The paramedic approached him first while the two firemen began assessing for imminent danger from any lingering cinders. "Are you okay?" asked the paramedic.

"I think so," Ralph responded.

"Can you tell me what happened?"

Ralph didn't want to get into the full story. The truth was he had just been terminated from his company at lunchtime. He came home, grabbed his trusty vices that always seem to come through when he needed to steady his nerves: a bottle of port wine and a Cohiba Churchill cigar. He then sat on the couch until he fell into a stupor. His cigar must have rolled off of the coffee table as it burned following his last drag, falling onto and igniting the area rug below. From there, the fire spread to his stacks of papers that were adorning practically his entire living room area. The living room and dining room were one conjoined room so he was lucky the fire had not spread further than it had in that short amount of time. Apparently, there was enough for the flames to consume in the 12 x 15 area. He was thankful he didn't have curtains, artwork, or other trinkets around the place.

In fact, Ralph had only moved into this apartment three months earlier after an argument—one of many over the last year—with his wife, Connie. Accusing Ralph of being married to his job, Connie had asked for a divorce several months previously. Neither one of them truly wanted to separate as they had been through so much together from several miscarriages to exciting assignments abroad, to the adoption of their son, Michael. In an attempt to salvage their deteriorating relationship, Ralph offered to move out with the hope of attending marriage counseling so they could get some space and eventually reconcile. However, he hadn't made it to even one session; the demands at work had been so great and he had been tasked with a new project that demanded even more hours at the office. It was in his career's best interest to be closer to the office given the late nights he needed to put in. After all, he reasoned, he was doing all of this to secure a comfortable future for his family. Why couldn't Connie understand that?

Today, his boss, Pete, called him in for a noontime meeting. No lunch was ordered and they weren't going out, which was odd, as Pete never missed a meal. And not simple meals either like cereal for breakfast or a sandwich for lunch. No, Pete had to have a hot meal with proper silverware and wait-staff service along with several courses and wine to near excess. To call a meeting at lunchtime without accompanying nourishment was unheard of. But, it never dawned on Ralph that the meeting would only last ten minutes or less, with Pete thanking Ralph for his eighteen years of exemplary service but they just had no room for him in the organization anymore.

Really?

***

"Sir?"

Ralph was ushered back into reality.

"Sir? Can you tell me what happened? I'd like to take you out to evaluate you for smoke inhalation," the paramedic insisted on taking Ralph's arm around his shoulder to brace him for support as he hoisted him to his feet. It was the first time Ralph could stand up without teetering to one side or tottering to the other.

"I'm fine. Really. I fell asleep. I should have put the cigar out. I made a bad decision," Ralph thought that wasn't the only bad decision he'd made recently.

The paramedic helped Ralph walk to the hallway of his apartment building, girding him with his left arm wrapped around his right shoulder. The two firemen had been listening in on Ralph's comments and followed him out the door as well.

It wasn't even four o'clock in the afternoon.

Chapter Two

The Disaster Worker

"Hi. I'm Steve. Are you okay?" he said as he handed Ralph a cup of piping hot coffee as well as a blanket emblazoned with the Red Cross logo on it. Ralph didn't realize how badly his hand was trembling, mostly out of shock for what just occurred, as he reached for the items. The enormity of what could have just transpired resonated within him as he almost spilled the dangerously hot coffee on him.

"Um, I think so."

Steve was a small-framed man in his mid-forties with brown eyes and long brown hair that was neatly pulled back into a ponytail so small, it didn't even make sense to have it pulled back. He couldn't help but stare at his bright red vest emblazoned with the letters "DAT". A small logo of the Red Cross adorned the vest over the upper left quadrant of his chest and a photo ID of a smiling face sat firmly in his transparent, right breast pocket. What looked to be a tool belt akin to the Tim "the tool man" Taylor on *Home Improvement* seemed to gobble up his waist. He noticed the walkie-talkie fastened to the belt along with a heavy set of keys and a clipboard with pen. He looked overburdened by apparati for his small frame.

"This day has completely sucked," Ralph mumbled underneath his breath.

"I'm sorry, I missed that. Beg your pardon?" Steve inquired.

"Nothing. I'm just having the worst day of my life," Ralph responded.

"Care to talk about it? We'll have a little bit of time together while we wait for the insurance adjusters, and your building manager will need you to sign off on the paperwork once she's spoken with the insurance company and the fire department. Part of my role is to help you clear away the clutter that you will surely encounter once your fire has been reported over the radio waves. You'll soon be overwhelmed with the number of people wanting you to sign up with them to fix, clean, adjust, move or restore your place. Plus, the insurance companies. It will be a lot for you to deal with right now and I'd like to make sure you understand your different options and which ones will work best for you. I am a non-partisan participant and can help you. Would you mind showing me a photo ID so I can get started on some of this paperwork?"

Ralph had no idea what he was talking about. All he could think of was how everything was gone. Poof. In an instant. The material things notwithstanding but his family, his career, his future. Things that three months earlier seemed to be on track. How had this happened?

If he was honest with himself, he knew that events at work were spiraling downward probably about a year or so ago. What with the new leadership coming on board in the company. Granted, sales had been sluggish if not downright negatively trending over the past three years. He and Connie had been stationed in Europe on a special assignment as an expat as part of his continued rise in leadership at the company. PhasInt was rapidly expanding in emerging markets and only top guns like Ralph were being asked to the dance to further their knowledge of the company and broaden the company's global footprint.

Previous to the recent economic downfall, PhasInt had experienced tremendous growth in the Asia Pacific markets while parts of Western Europe and the US were stagnating. The next great horizon for the company was south of the border and should this first international assignment go well, executive management might determine that Ralph could be the right cultural and professional fit for continued professional acceleration.

Ralph had proven himself over the last eighteen years with the company, holding positions of greater authority and responsibility from entry level analyst to senior advisor to team lead to department manager to comptroller. Knowing he needed to diversify his talent base, he took on financial projects that allowed him to dabble in operations and sales. He proactively and willingly reached out to other departments to learn more about how he and his department could help drive overall profits, all the while educating others outside of finance how what they did, what they bought, and who they hired had a direct impact to the bottom line. In a few words, he was a company man who couldn't believe his fortune of landing another great job time and time again.

During his tenure with PhasInt, Ralph had seen forays into international expansion. Given their humble beginnings as a domestic lending institution, PhasInt had grown to become a major player in the world of micro-financing for small start ups. The overseas markets were the next waves of opportunity and Ralph had vocalized to his superiors and colleagues how he would be interested in learning more about the international markets. While not officially overseeing the financial accounting for any of the smaller sub-divisions abroad, Ralph made it a point to ensure collegiality and collaboration with his offshore counterparts—they could always come to him when they had a question about the general accounting practices and principles that he'd drafted and revised over the years.

Thus, he was delighted to have been offered the opportunity to represent his company abroad and jumped at the chance after talking it over with his wife. In this new role, he would become the divisional general manager—a role he relished that would give him P&L responsibility, access to offshore operations, and oversight of hundreds of local employees. It also placed him in a prime position to return to HQ at an entirely elevated executive level. Even Connie was excited to experience a new culture and country, given her college studies in international relations.

They had moved overseas and put everything at home in storage, knowing that their assignment was temporary and they would be back after his contractual term of three years was up. Indeed, they were back in Philadelphia sooner than expected given the changing leadership in the organization.

He received the call on a Wednesday afternoon to be in Philadelphia Thursday evening for a dinner with one of the owners. A flurry of activity ensued to get Ralph on the morning British Airways flight direct to the city of brotherly love by four pm which would give him just enough time to drop his items off at the Sheraton, freshen up and meet the Chairman for six pm. When he got the call, he had no idea that the company would be calling him back for an 'exciting, special project' that needed his unique blend of global leadership and financial acuity. He, Connie, and Michael would need to move back to the States within thirty days. Ralph worked diligently over the last month to tie up every project he had initiated to ensure a smooth transition to his not-quite-ready hand-picked successor whom he'd been grooming since his arrival day.

Ralph had envisioned this day in coming but not before his three-year term ran out. The decision meant that he would need to accelerate the training and development of his local teams so they could assume their new positions of leadership in 1/3 less time than anticipated. While the moment was bittersweet for Ralph and his family, he was elated that his local team would be receiving the opportunity to advance themselves and their careers. In fact, despite the economic turbulence out of the US headquarters, the smaller, offshore divisions of PhasInt had been experiencing double digit growth year over year. Moving back to the US meant less flexibility and independence given the challenging finances. Regardless, coming back to HQ after a successful expat stint clearly demonstrated Ralph's acumen and ability to lead, develop, and synergize teams of diverse make ups as well as afforded him greater exposure internally.

Ralph oftentimes felt that living outside the US hub meant less exposure to opportunities for advancement and development.

Similarly, Ralph tried to create an equal harmony in his home although admittedly, most of that work fell to Connie. Thankfully, the end of the school term was drawing near so stress on the family would be minimized and Connie and Michael began the process of saying goodbye to friends made in a foreign setting. Right on schedule, Ralph made it back on a plane to the US within thirty days when he found himself sitting across from the company owners on his first day back at HQ.

Ralph had always tried to foster a positive relationship with the owners. Granted, he was several levels removed from them but his performance and loyalty spoke for itself, or so he thought. Greeted by one of the "Trinity", as many called the trio of owners of the privately held company, as he walked through the frosted glass doors on his first day back, Ralph learned that due to increasing economic demands, the privately held company was looking at investment by private equity who intended to bring in an outside CEO. It was determined that by hiring an external executive who had previous turn-around experience, they could reverse the downward turn in revenues and right the company back to profitable splendor. Ralph was told that his return to the HQ was part of an initiative to return all expats home and replace them with local talent who were groomed for exactly this occasion.

Vaughn, the primary shareholder of the firm, firmly grasped Ralph's hand and bellowed, "Welcome back Ralph. You did a fine job in Europe. But, we need you here. As you know projections are down and with your well rounded repertoire within the organization, we need you to work on a special project for us. In fact, you will be reporting directly to the new CFO who will be coming on board in the next two weeks." Ralph was certainly flattered by the individual attention and opportunity to shine at an executive level.

Vaughn continued, "Challenging times need leaders who can traverse the terrain with ease, finesse, and sophistication. We will be unveiling this new management team at an executive committee meeting held this Friday. We will be sending out an announcement tomorrow about the various entrances and departures of our executive management teams. Knowing that you had strong relationships and performance in US Finance, it only made sense to bring you back to infuse stability and confidence within the organization."

"Thank you, sir. I will do my best and will get started right away. Tell me more about the team I'll be leading and what your vision and objectives for this project will be," Ralph beamed with pride.

"The team will be just you. You will need to work on a transition plan with the new CFO to bring him up to speed on both our US operations as well as our overseas divisions. There is nobody in the organization who quite knows the ins and outs of our successes and failures like you do, particularly on the finance side. Consider this a prime opportunity for visibility and leadership at an executive level," posed Vaughn. A few other details were shared which led to more questions than answers, although Ralph dared not ask Vaughn right now. Where were the current CEO and CFO going? Who else was going with them? How long had this been in the works? Who else knew? What did it mean for him? Ralph shook off the initial feeling of confusion and uncertainty regarding his place within the newly emerging company. After all, he had been personally tapped to not only shadow but also teach the new, incoming CFO, right? Did it really matter if he no longer had P&L responsibility or if a team of employees reported directly to him?

***

"I didn't catch your name, sir? Also, I need to see some photo identification so I can get started on the paperwork to help you," Steve jolted Ralph out of his private thoughts. He had seen this distant and vacant look in clients' eyes before. To Steve, Ralph appeared despondent, mentally replaying the events of the previous hour in his mind. He pulled out his clipboard and pen.

"I'm Ralph. Ralph Pibbs. What does DAT stand for?"

"Disaster Action Team. I am one of several qualified individuals who are amongst the first responders for the American Red Cross when we hear of a disaster occurring in the city. It could be a fire, like this, or it could be a building collapse, a water main break, or another event that displaces families from their homes. It's my duty to share with you the resources that are available to you right now since you won't be able to return to your dwelling place immediately while it is being renovated and repaired."

Ugh. He hadn't thought of the fact that he would not be permitted to re-enter his apartment until a proper investigation and thorough renovation of the premises had been completed. It looked like only surface damage to the carpeting, floor, and furniture but he knew Steve was right.

"How long before you think I can return?" Ralph asked.

"It's hard to say. It depends on how much damage was caused to the floor and walls. A full structural analysis will need to be completed. Plus, for sure you've got smoke damage within your apartment and maybe to your neighbors," Steve responded.

"I saw my neighbors and they didn't say anything about their apartments. I assume they were okay. I mean, it was a fire sure but it wasn't like a full blaze," Ralph tried to downplay the situation.

"You don't know what damage was done to the apartment beneath you or the one on top of you. Think of the smoke that wafted upwards and the damage caused to the floor. There may be structural damage to the floor and maybe even to any electrical wiring that runs through the ceiling in the apartment beneath you," Steve continued.

"As DAT lead for our Friday team, I've seen all too often how a 'simple' fire really has farther reaching consequences that affects not just the site of the origin of the fire but adjacent apartments as well. You'll likely be out for at least a few days. Look, here comes some of the restoration companies' personnel now," Steve motioned to an athletically built, younger man entering the apartment foyer.

He approached Steve with outstretched hand, "HI. I'm John from Clean-All Restoration Services. I understand there's been a fire in the building?" He turned to look at Ralph. "Did the fire originate in your apartment?" Ralph sheepishly nodded.

"I'm sorry to hear that, sir. My company performs restoration services that will get your place cleaned up in no time. I brought some brochures with me that explain how our process works. In a time like this, it's best to put your trust in an established company who has a reputation for care, completeness and confidentiality."

Without missing a beat, John continued his spiel. "In fact, we have restored over 200 homes in the Philadelphia region. Don't you owe it to yourself to hire a company who is going to return you to your home in as quick and safe a manner as possible?"

Steve jumped in. "John, I don't think now is a good time to speak with Mr. Pibbs. The building manager is still upstairs with the firemen assessing the damage. Perhaps it's best for you to wait in the building manager's office?"

"Good idea. I wasn't sure if he was a renter or if this was a condominium building where each tenant owns their own unit." John seemed to speak to Steve as if Ralph was no longer in the room. With that, John was on his way, nary giving Ralph another look.

"What was that about?" asked a bewildered Ralph.

"There will be more of them. The service these companies provide is absolutely necessary to get you back into your place in a safe and efficient manner but the tactics they employ to acquire business can sometimes be questionable, especially if you don't already have renters or homeowners insurance. It's like they are ambulance chasers," explained Steve. "But, in this case, they are fire truck chasers. They often times listen in on the radio, picking up reports of fires that occur throughout the city hoping to be the first one to the scene so they can extol the virtues of their services and take advantage of your compromised mental state right now."

"Don't they realize that I have no idea what has just happened or the extent of the damage?" prodded Ralph.

"Indeed they do. They are counting on the fact that you are in an emotionally fragile state of mind and have no idea what you need right now. Like I said, the services they perform are absolutely necessary to get you back in your home in as little time as possible. It's just that their business development tactics are lacking, um, a certain level of panache and sensitivity. Given that there are over seven hundred fires occurring within the city every year, you would think they would improve their demeanor during a time like this."

"Boy, I'll say. Seven hundred fires a year? That's roughly two a day. What happens to all those people?" Ralph wondered aloud.

"Well, oftentimes people can't return to their homes—much like you. So, they need a place to stay if they don't already have relatives or friends with whom they can stay temporarily. First things first. Let's get started on the paperwork which begins with production of a valid ID. You obviously can't go back up to your apartment until it's cleaned and fully certified with a certificate of occupancy stating that you can go back. Do you have a place to stay until that time?"

There was no way he could call Connie and tell her that not only did he lose his job but that he'd almost burned down his apartment causing him to be without shelter and needed to come home. There were too many other issues for them to work out and he knew he hadn't devoted any time to their relationship since he moved out; working on this so-called 'special project' had seemed to consume all his time, energy, and thoughts since moving back home from Europe. To call her now at this point was just too humiliating for him and would likely be insulting to her—the only reason he needed to come home was because he had no other place to stay. He would have to stay in a hotel for the next couple of nights until his apartment was ready and he was prepared to share the debilitating news about his job.

Ralph realized that his wallet was amongst the items he had casually tossed on the coffee table, near the pile of papers that went up in a puff.

"Damn it!" He didn't mean for his words to be so audible.

"What? What's wrong?" Steve probed.

"I just realized my wallet was in the fire. I don't have any money. No ID. No credit cards. Ugh, and all my information for the banks, loyalty rewards programs, everything—they are in my computer and Blackberry at work. I have no way to get access to that information right now." Ralph started to realize the enormity of his situation which spanned more than just a rug-consuming fire.

Steve pulled out his cell phone from the many attachments on his tool belt and extended it to him. "Here. Call work and see if they can extract that information for you."

Ralph refused to take the phone. "I can't. I got fired today. They took my laptop and have probably already wiped it clean since they took it at noon and escorted me out of the building. I can't call my boss and ask him to read me the information from my private files. I should have downloaded all of my personal information before this happened. In fact, I should have never kept anything personal on my computer in the first place. I just didn't see this coming. I didn't see any of this coming," Ralph was trying to hold in his emotion.

"I am so sorry Mr. Pibbs. I had no idea about your extenuating circumstances. Look, I will bring you to the Red Cross House. It's a short drive away from here and it's where most people go when they have no other alternative after a disaster strikes. They will provide you with everything you need while your apartment is cleaned up. They've got private suites with private bathrooms, a small kitchen and dining area. Really, you'll be very comfortable there until you develop a plan and timeline to resume your life again. Do you have a way to get there or would you like a ride?"

***

Resume his life again? Was that possible? Did Steve not realize what had just transpired over the last year? The last three months? Heck, over the last four hours? Ralph's mind raced to the image of walking out the door of PhasInt escorted by the hired security guards.

Amazing how an eighteen-year career of esteemed and loyal service comes to a tarnished end simply for being at the wrong place at the wrong time, Ralph thought.

After Pete closed the door behind him at noon today, Ralph saw the head of HR, Lee, seated at the side table. Ralph went to shake his hand but was met with a cold, "Have a seat, Ralph." Lee didn't extend his hand to Ralph but rather used it to motion to him to sit at the small round table that was partially blocked from outside views looking in.

Pete began, "Ralph, you know we brought you back from Europe a few months ago with the all-important task of inducting our new CFO to the business. You've had a wonderful career here at PhasInt but there just doesn't seem to be a place in the new organization for you. I'm sorry but this is just not working out for us any longer."

"Am I being terminated?" a bewildered Ralph exclaimed. He'd never been fired before. He'd never even gotten a negative performance review. In fact, he had not once received a piece of detrimental coaching from anyone above him; he had always received glowing reviews about his attention to details, his loyalty, and his ability to get the job done. This couldn't be happening.

Lee chimed in, "Don't take this personally, Ralph. The organization has grown in tremendous ways and at this juncture, your position is being eliminated. There will be an exit package for you," as he slid a manila envelope towards Ralph. "Take some time this weekend looking over the paperwork. Feel free to call or email me with any questions you might have. You will have twenty-one days to provide us a response and we will take it from there. You know how to reach me, right?"

Ralph felt a lump in his throat and was at a loss for words. He arose, grabbed his folio that he'd brought with him on which to take notes as well as the envelope, and turned to walk out the door. "Can I fetch some items from my office?"

"Not at this moment, Ralph. Given your prominence in the organization as well as access to sensitive company information, we can't permit you to gain entry to your office or your computer. We will have one of the administrative staff box up your personal items and have them couriered to your home next week," countered Lee. Pete sat expressionless and motionless in the corner, his baby blue eyes following the exchange between former executive and HR.

As Ralph went to twist the door handle to let himself out, Pete arose and approached Ralph. Ralph couldn't bear to look him in the eye and did not see Pete's hand outstretched to shake his, which nervously grabbed for the door. It would not dawn on Ralph until later that no one during this entire process uttered a "thank you", handshake, or pat on the back for anything and all that Ralph had done for the company.

Upon exiting the office, Ralph was immediately met by the uniformed security personnel who regularly sat at the executive reception checking everyone's badges. "I'll walk you out, sir," said the guard.

Ralph couldn't acknowledge the guard but kept walking straight for the elevators and ultimately the reception lobby. The only thing he recognized and was thankful for was the fact that at lunchtime on Fridays, PhasInt always catered a hot meal to the employees; everyone on the seventh floor was in the lunchroom on the fifth. Preferring to keep his head down as he walked out the door of only the second company he had ever known, Ralph walked the eight blocks back to his apartment barely noticing anything or anyone.

***

"Mr. Pibbs? Would you like a ride to the Red Cross House?" Steve seemed adamant about getting an answer from him as his mind wandered afar.

"How far away is it? I can probably walk. The fresh air might do me good."

"It's about 30 blocks but really, it's no bother. I have the van with me and it will just take us fifteen minutes to get there with this Friday afternoon traffic. Let me call them and let them know to expect you."

Steve walked to the other side of the apartment lobby to make the call. He came back after three or five minutes. Ralph wasn't really sure. Time seemed to be a blur to him right now. What time was it right now anyway? He went to look at his watch but realized that he'd taken that off, too, when he sat on the couch and started drinking. He would be pissed if he learned that indeed his Tag Hueur had been consumed in the blaze. Or worse, stolen by one of the various people who had already been in or will be in his apartment over the coming days.

Steve noticed him looking at a bare swatch of skin on his left forearm. "It's almost five o'clock. I just saw the building manager come back down and you'll need to sign some papers before we can go. Once you are done with that, I can take you over to the House. You will be there just in time for dinner. I'll pull the van around and meet you outside when you're ready."

Dinner? He certainly had no appetite for food. In fact, he had no appetite for anything other than falling into a coma and sleeping until he woke up from this nightmare.

"Hey, Mr. Pibbs," beckoned the building manager. "I need you to sign some papers. Thankfully, the damage isn't as bad as it could have been. You're very lucky." All Ralph could muster was a low grumble. She motioned for him to enter her office and sit on the chair facing her small, wooden desk that was piled high with applications, permits, and invoices. If cleanliness was the next thing to Godliness, this office was certainly on the border of purgatory.

She handed Ralph a letter that absolved the apartment complex from liability should Ralph's rental insurance not cover the full damages. An investigation was underway which would be completed shortly and Ralph would need to find temporary housing while his apartment was being assessed and cleaned. Her explanation of events to come during the next week was exactly as Steve prescribed.

Ralph took a blue pen out of the US Army mug that sat on her desk that was overflowing with pens, pencils, rulers, and markers, and shakily signed his name.

"Did you happen to see my wallet upstairs?" Ralph was hopeful.

"It's not my job to look for it, but apparently you had a lot of paper that went up like kindling. Everything around the area rug, the coffee table, and the couch is pretty much destroyed. You know, lit cigars and papers don't make great partners," her attempt at sarcastic humor wasn't appreciated. She did, however, have a replacement key to the apartment for him. She held it up to his face. "Here's your replacement key. You can't use it until your apartment is cleared. I'll call you when it's ready."

"You can't call me. I don't have my phone," Ralph retorted.

"Fine then. You call me from wherever you are and I'll let you know if it's ready that day," giving him a bit of south Philly atty-tood.

Ralph grabbed the key, handed the papers back to her, got up from the chair, and turned to walk out of her office.

"Do you have a place to stay? We are at full occupancy here. I think the Red Cross guy is helping you find a place, right?" Ralph was convinced the building manager was asking more out of being nosy than out of genuine concern for his well being.

"I'll be fine," Ralph shot back.

With that, he walked out the door to meet Steve who was waiting for him outside.

Chapter Three

The Drive

True to his word, Steve pulled up to the vestibule area in a white, twelve seat passenger van, emblazoned with the words "American Red Cross" across the side. He rolled down the passenger window and shouted, "Hop in. I'll get you there in a jiffy." Ralph politely obliged and settled into the cold, front seat.

He snapped the seat belt in the buckle and asked, "So, how did you get involved in this line of work anyway?"

Steve placed the gear into drive and slowly accelerated out of the delivery area of the apartment building. He seemed to take his time, both in navigating the city streets that were bustling with people leaving work for the weekend and ready to spend quality time with their families, as well as in answering his question.

"I actually just started doing this about a few months ago. It's always been a passion of mine to direct disaster operations and when I was laid off in a massive reorganizational effort about a year ago, I took the time to reflect on what I wanted out of my career and my future. Being part of a high performing team was something that was really important to me when I got right down to it and sketched out my values, passions, and professional desires."

"You mean, you were fired, too? What did you do before doing this?" Ralph imagined he must have taken a massive pay cut to drive a van around the city picking up those who likely could never pay him back. Besides, wasn't the Red Cross a non-profit? Those people don't make that much. Ralph was intrigued to hear more of his story.

"I prefer to think of it as a downsizing. My reporting lines had changed six times over two years and knew that when my company merged with another similarly sized organization that it would only be a matter of time before my department and position were made redundant. I was in operations for a pharmaceutical giant and had been there just a few years and the next logical step would have been a VP of supply chain but those jobs go to where the manufacturing is. Moving was not a compromise my family was willing to make."

"Who did you work for?" Ralph inquired.

"You know, all the big players you've certainly heard of before. Lots of mergers and acquisitions going on. They can't keep everybody so I knew my time was coming to an end. I had a lot of conversations with many of the remaining executives to see what my options were and what they could do to help me. The typical response was "We respect what you've done for the company but there is nothing we can do". So, I stayed in my leadership position until the final day my entire team knew we were all leaving. I spent my last months setting my team and those who survived up for success. Leaving on a positive note was important for several reasons."

"So, what happened?" Ralph wanted to hear the story. In a twisted way, it actually felt good to hear that someone else had experienced the pain of losing a job.

"Actually, what happened isn't really important anymore. It might have been for the first six months but it's not anymore even though the shock of being downsized resonates in you. While it was no surprise to any of us, it's a feeling of disbelief that you have to deal with, especially as people in the organization start treating you differently. You become branded as "one of those" and I really felt for my team of seventy—only six were going to stay with the company after the merger. I tried to help many of them land new positions by writing letters on their behalf, conducting reference calls, and making connections for them within GPSEG. I didn't really dedicate myself to finding a new position for a few months as I felt completely responsible for my team. My wife was pretty annoyed with me since I was helping others find jobs and nothing for me.

Ahhh, the old bird got over it eventually. She's happy I finally got a job I enjoy. And, I still got to be true to my team. Yeah, she's a keeper," Steve winked while glancing over at Ralph.

Ralph didn't understand what he meant by GPSEG but said nothing.

Steve continued, "So, I went on a number of interviews and actually turned down a few as I knew they were not right for me. I didn't want to just rebound into another frying pan and now, I have a new calling. A new passion. I wish I had capitalized on this realization earlier. But, it all came about when I earnestly started looking at my talents—what I was gifted at—and matching them up with my interests. I thought I was pretty good in operations; I could envision what my company and clients wanted and design protocols and procedures to meet those needs. I am also extremely detail oriented and like working with a diverse group of people. But, more than that, being part of a team is what makes me tick. I guess that's why I got into pharmaceuticals and healthcare; I was surrounded by high achievers who were dedicated toward a common cause. That's the basis for a great team. In a small way, I also felt like I was making a difference in people's lives at some level and contributing to their overall quality of life."

Pursue Your Passions

Steve was clearly on a roll. "Yeah, it's been really exciting since I had that revelation last year. I wanted to help people. I wanted to meet them where they were at during times of need. The Red Cross seemed like a great fit as I am able to use my talents of approaching others, listening to their needs, and helping to solve an issue they might not necessarily be able to on their own. Plus, I get to meet a lot of unique and fascinating people throughout our fair city. That's important to me. I need to be involved and I need to be a part of a great team."

Ralph marveled at how Steve lit up as he talked about his passion for leading a dynamic team. His voice was raised; he talked faster; his smile broadened; and his eyes widened. This was genuinely the look of a person engaged in and fully alive with his work. In fact, he mused whether he even considered this "work" in the truest sense of the word.

"You really enjoy what you do," Ralph stated the obvious.

"Without a doubt! I don't know if I will be doing this for the rest of my career but I am thoroughly enjoying this experience. And, it will be a great springboard for me to develop new skills that can be parlayed into an entirely new repertoire for me, should I so choose. The important thing is that I chose something that worked in so many dimensions of my life whereas I may have made unconscious trade-offs in the past. Granted, I took a massive pay cut but you know what? I've never been happier or more fulfilled in all my life. Looking back now, after having had a year to ponder what's happened, I wouldn't have it any other way. I wake up every day, not knowing the circumstances that I will face or the people that I will meet but I do know one thing."

"What's that?" Ralph encouraged him to continue.

"That I am fulfilled and I am thankful. I really can't ask for anything more than that," Steve smiled broadly.

***

Ralph couldn't think of the last time he was really fulfilled or thankful. Sure, he had had good times in the various positions he had held throughout his career but could he say he was 'fulfilled'? The money had been great and ever since he graduated with his degree in business, making money was really the only thing that mattered to him and he progressively increased his income year over year. He had found and married the girl of his dreams and, after several years of trying to get pregnant and experiencing devastating miscarriages, they finally had a son they called their own.

His mind wandered back to the last time he saw his son at his little league game. "Put your whole body into the swing, Michael!" Ralph recalls calling out, trying not to sound too proud and not to sound too judgmental. He wasn't one of those weekend baseball dads who would occasionally receive dirty glances from the other parents. To be at that level meant that he would have had to be involved in his son's activities; various projects at work and the new CFO had him missing most of those games. Fulfilled?

He wished he had spent more time coaching Michael how to throw the ball or steal a base or swing the bat. Then again, how could he when he hadn't worked out or kept up with his own fitness routine and goals since moving out of the States. It sometimes prevented him from being the kind of involved father he would have liked to be to Michael and he truly did feel an overwhelming joy when he was with the boy. Granted, most of the time physically spent with his son and wife were alternately spent with his mind elsewhere. The closing month end reports. The sales commissions payouts. The timeliness of the accounts receivables. It was a never-ending cycle of work that continually stayed at the forefront of Ralph's mind.

The last time he saw Michael was two weeks ago as he had promised to take him to a Phillies game on a Sunday afternoon. Connie had asked him to spend the full day that Sunday with them starting with meeting at church, to then lunch afterward, to the Phillies game. He just couldn't muster up the courage to attend church again yet. It wasn't in him to act the hypocrite and show up with smiley faces pretending that everything in their family was fine and dandy when in truth they were separated and living apart. Appearances were important, sure, but he did not have it in him to deceive God in His dwelling place. He didn't care what the Joneses thought, and for as much of a jerk as Connie had told him he was, he still did care what God thought.

Instead, he met Connie and Michael at the local Cheesecake Factory in King of Prussia. Connie had always loved the fish tacos, and who could resist the cheesecakes? Plus, it was busy and noisy enough there that he did not have to attempt too much small talk. As their beeper went off indicating their table was ready, Michael saw some neighborhood friends of his at another table. Ralph just waved to the parents; he couldn't remember their names and didn't feel like going over to chitchat.

"What time do you think the game will be over?" Connie asked as they settled into their booth.

"I'm not sure. You know how baseball games are. But, I do have a call with Australia tonight at 7 so I'll need to leave the stadium at five to ensure I get Michael home by six so that I can be back at my place for the call," Ralph responded.

"So, you're not even going to stay for the entire game? Ralph, that's not fair. You know Mikey has been looking forward to this game and to spending time with you for weeks. You always seem to let him down," Connie countered.

The guilt set in and Ralph restrained himself to keep his anger in check. Between clenched teeth he hissed, "Damn it, Connie, I am doing the best that I can. I told him I would take him to a game and I am. You know I have this major project I am working on and I need to be available when the team needs me. Seven p.m. my time is nine a.m. Sydney time. I need to show that I am flexible and amenable to the needs of the team. This is a great opportunity for me to show the new CFO my full span of control and understanding of our business. I don't know why you just can't understand and cut me some slack."

At this point, Michael returned to the table of his parents' right after Connie muttered, "Just drop it. I'm sick and tired of Michael and I always being the ones who have to compromise."

***

A loud honk from a taxicab behind them brought him back to the conversation with Steve. He looked nonplussed by the toot and slowly eased his foot on the pedal to accelerate off of Market Street.

"That's great to love what you do. How did you arrive at this juncture? I mean, volunteer work is very different than corporate life. Didn't you find it to be a difficult transition?" Ralph prodded him.

"Well, it's interesting you say that. And, while the Red Cross accomplishes its mission through the mobilization of volunteers and generosity of its donors, I'm actually a paid staff member. In fact, I oversee operations for the entire Philadelphia region. And, my transition was facilitated by a great coach who inspired me to come to this conclusion. Being in operations within the pharmaceutical industry can get a little, well, shall we say, incestuous? So, moving from one company to another is pretty easy and you come to know a lot of your colleagues, peers and competitors, particularly when bigger companies are buying out the smaller ones which was the case for me in the later stages of my career. So, when I was finally let go last year, my company offered me an outplacement firm and career coach as part of my separation package," Steve explained.

Ralph wondered to himself if he was offered the same thing. He hadn't even bothered to look inside the manila envelope that Lee had handed to him a few hours ago. In fact, where was that envelope? He would have to search for it once he was allowed back inside his apartment. For now, though, he wanted to hear more from Steve.

"Really? I wasn't aware that companies gave such perks to lower level employees," Ralph's words trickled from his head to his mouth without thinking.

"I wasn't a 'lower level employee'," Steve shot back. "I oversaw all of the operational activities for a global corporation with offshore manufacturing and sourcing as well as a strong brand presence in international markets."

"Sorry. I assumed you would not have voluntarily chosen to go from being an executive at a multi-national firm to do something so…simple," Ralph couldn't stop the flow of words from his mouth. He really didn't mean it as an insult but if this guy really did what he said he did, why was he doing what he's doing now?

Engage a Trusted Business Advisor, Coach, or Respected Ally

Steve seemed to have read his mind. "Well, as I was saying, my company offered me the option of working with an outplacement firm and career coach. I couldn't wait to get started with them the Monday following my Friday departure. Having never been in this situation before or even looking for a job in two decades, the outplacement services were extraordinarily helpful in the early days such as helping me re-write my resume. They also tried to tease out of me the specifics in terms of getting the evidence presented on paper which was very helpful in crafting out what was next for me. Plus, the educational and online programs were tailored to bringing me to where I am now. I even got a personal coach to meet with me in person once and the rest of the times on the phone or the internet."

Steve paused long enough to wave a pedestrian halfway through the crosswalk to make it to the other end of the street. "One thing I did not fully understand with outplacement firms and coaching groups, however, is that they don't find jobs for you. It was nothing like that actually. What you get is someone who is willing to give you instruction on how you can conduct your search. This is a vast distinction and sometimes a rude awakening when you realize you are on your own. Not that it's bad, it's just different and you have to align your expectations accordingly. For me and my coach, as I had done some charity work in the past and after taking a number of assessments through the outplacement firm, I had rank ordered my preferences for what to do next."

"What were your rankings?" Ralph inquired.

"One, I could certainly go back into the corporate world. It's what I was familiar with and knew lots of people in the industry. Two, I could go into management consulting as so many of my peers had done in the past. With so many organizations downsizing over the last five years, there are a lot of individual players out there offering their consulting wares. Three, I could venture out on my own with a boutique firm but I'm really not into being an individual performer—I like to be a part of something bigger than myself. Or, the last option my coach and I came up with is to work in the non-profit sector utilizing my already polished skill set in operations. We jointly determined that my values were tied to community. But, you can't be a part of a community if you are traveling all the time. To be really engaged and active, you have to be physically available. By having a career that had me traveling all the time, I was actually disengaged from community. It was also hard to connect with relationships, which is something I valued but didn't act out. So, my coach and I determined that my operational background and skills would be hugely successful and welcomed at a large scale non-profit where I had the opportunity to interact hands on with clients and other employees. Thankfully, there are lots of those on the East Coast and I'm having the time of my life. I may not have arrived at this decision on my own without the help of that coach."

"That's quite a story. It sounds quite the opposite of what that renovation company guy was trying to do to me a few minutes ago—take advantage of an unfortunate situation," Ralph noticed.

"Exactly! That's why I tell you amongst the first things in your transition into and out of unemployment is to align yourself with trusted guides and mentors to help you arrive at an articulation of your passion, if you don't already know it," Steve chirped as he slammed on brakes to avoid hitting a bicycle messenger who had just cut in front of him.

Chapter Four

The Intake

He hadn't paid much attention to the turns they were taking as they drove through the city to reach the Red Cross House but he could tell that they were in University City simply based on the number of young people out and about. It was still afternoon on a Friday so the students from Drexel, Penn and Temple were likely finishing up classes for the day, heading back to their dorms or apartments, and preparing for a big night out on the town.

His mind flashed to his fond memories of his own college days at Ohio State University. He met Connie at a fraternity party. She was a freshman, he was a senior. She looked so sweet during the mixer with the Sigma Mu Gamma sorority and had the most genuine smile and sparkly eyes.

Never one lacking confidence, he approached her with his trusty line, "Hi. I'm Ralph." It put him out there but was non-committal. After all, he wasn't anticipating to marry her, just get to know her.

"Hi, I'm Connie. Do you belong to this fraternity?" she asked.

"Yes, in fact, I'm the treasurer. Do you belong to Sigma Mu?" Ralph continued her lead of the conversation.

"I'm just rushing. I'm not sure if I will join. I mean, the school is so big that it'd be nice to have a set of ready-made and reliable friends. But, I'm just checking it out and participating in the mixers and such. There are only two of us from my high school here so I thought it would be good to get to meet new people. Where are you from?" Connie obviously had no issue keeping up a conversation and while Ralph couldn't recall every bit of their first conversation, he did learn quite a bit about her that evening: from Ohio, had an older brother, her father was a high school football coach and gym teacher, her mom a nurse's aide. She wanted to study international relations even though her parents believed it might not be a marketable degree unless she continued with her studies and went to law school. By the end of the evening, he had gotten her phone number and was delighted when, after calling her the next day, she agreed to go out with him the following weekend.

They dated exclusively for the remainder of the school year until Ralph graduated and took a job in Cleveland at a small brokerage firm. He was still a few hours from Connie and they were able to continue their courtship on the weekends. Within eighteen months, a job offer with PhasInt, a financial services firm, took him away to their headquarters in Philadelphia where he was to be an entry-level analyst. Wanting to make a good impression for his new bosses, Ralph regularly put in 12 hour plus days and, as Connie was finishing up her junior year, the long distance provided both an opportunity to grow in new ways. With only another year and a half left to go in school, Connie made the decision to join Ralph in Philadelphia, thus putting her degree and potential dreams of law school on hold. They married in June right after her junior year.

***

As Steve turned into the parking lot and pulled the van to a stop, Ralph was jolted out of his trip down memory lane. He noticed that adjacent to the small parking lot looked to be a large, college-style dormitory for students.

"We're here. Don't worry about not having your personal items with you. LaShaun at the front desk will arrange to provide you with the toiletries, clothes, linens, and anything else you'll need during your stay." Steve sounded a little too chipper and optimistic for him.

They both opened their doors at the same time to step out of the van with Steve then getting out and opening up the back seat to remove his clipboard and what looked to be like a toolbox. Ralph shut his door and walked empty-handed toward the front of the building.

Across the top of the entrance was emblazoned "RED CROSS HOUSE" in bold, black letters.

Steve overtook him in opening up the door, held it open for Ralph to walk through and proceeded up to the front desk.

"Hi LaShaun. I've got Mr. Pibbs here. He will be staying with us for the next few nights. Can you put him up in a single room?"

LaShaun smiled at Steve and then at Ralph. "Sure thing. We've been expecting him. I have a single room on the second floor. I can show him right up after I receive your paperwork from you. Mr. Pibbs? Would you care to have a seat in our foyer area?" LaShaun seemed appropriately pleasant and poised in her tone. Not too much sympathy yet just enough emotion to make Ralph feel like she's seen people with his circumstances before.

Ralph turned around and went to sit on the forest green cloth sofa adorning the foyer area when he noticed some of the pictures festooning the walls. Within what seemed to be seconds of departing the reception desk, Ralph noticed Steve exchange pleasantries and paperwork with LaShaun before heading back over to Ralph. Steve acknowledged Ralph's glancing over the artwork.

"LaShaun has got you all taken care of. She will show you to your room and shortly you'll be visited by a case worker who can help you sort out everything that you'll be needing over the next couple of days to help you get back on your feet," Steve put his hand in his vest pocket, extracted a business card, wrote something on the back and then stuck out his hand in a gesture to quickly say goodbye while handing Ralph the card.

Confused, Ralph clasped Steve's hand in his and asked, "Where are you going? Who is going to meet me? How long am I going to stay here? I don't even have a phone with me." Ralph was cut off before he could ask his next question.

"I've got to go respond to another emergency happening in the city but don't worry. The caseworker is actually on site right now. You're lucky the weekend hasn't fully sprung upon us otherwise you'd have to wait until Monday to see someone," Steve continued. "I think it's Laura but I'm not 100% sure. Whoever it is, I guarantee you that you will get everything you need to get through this trying ordeal, Mr. Pibbs. You'll be in good hands. You'll be fine."

"Thanks for your help, Steve. I guess it's like you said, you are helping me engage trusted allies right now. I appreciate that. I don't even know where to begin," stammered Ralph who could no longer maintain eye contact with Steve.

"You've already started engaging with trusted advisors and mentors. Now, find your passion and follow it," and with that, Steve turned on his heels, walked out the door, and hopped back into his van.

***

As the door closed behind Steve, Ralph looked down at the card. The Red Cross logo appeared in the top left hand corner and Steve's name, title and phone number were printed across the center front. Turning the card over, Ralph saw that Steve wrote in capital letters:

- PASSION
- ALLIES

He looked at the card until the letters blurred in his eyes.

"Mr. Pibbs?" LaShaun called out to Ralph.

"Yes?"

"Hi. I'm LaShaun. I will be showing you to your room right now. Do you have any belongings with you?"

"Uh, no," Ralph felt humiliated knowing that she did not intend that to be his reaction. He'd never felt so reduced to…nothing.

"Oh, no worries, sir. We've got some clothes you can go through in our warehouse area downstairs when your caseworker comes for you. She should be finished with her current client shortly. Let me show you to your room where you can wait for her. Please follow me," LaShaun arose from her seat and offered him a warm smile. Ralph believed she seemed genuinely concerned and kind, judging by the intentional gaze to meet his eyes.

They both walked silently down the hall to the left of the reception area to take an elevator to the second floor. Ralph had no desire to engage in conversation so he simply followed her dutifully after exiting the lift and walking straight down the hall. He mentally remarked how his initial instinct was correct upon arrival when he thought he was entering a dormitory. Doors on either side of the hallway bore a number and the walls were painted a muted yellow. Artwork, similar to what he'd seen downstairs, was carefully placed on the walls. Some were behind glass frames, others not.

A door opened up just as they passed by and out walked a spirited youngster totally bedecked in variations of purple from her sparkly royal purple tutu to her lavender leggings, plum colored shirt and colorful beads in her hair. "I'll be right back, mommy," she called inside the door, nary giving he nor LaShaun a glance.

"I'm coming with you," said apparently the mom who appeared just as quickly out the door as her daughter.

"I'll race you to the stairs, mommy! 'Scuse me!" as she burst by Ralph and LaShaun toward the end of the corridor which seemed to be where the staircase was located. The little girl's laughter could be heard echoing throughout the corridor. Ralph mused to himself how it was nice to hear laughter today. In fact, it was the first time he had.

"Pardon me," said the mom as she swiftly walked by both them, trying to keep up with her lively child.

LaShaun stopped at the next door from mother and daughter marked "25", inserted the key, and turned the doorknob.

"And, we are here. You should have everything you need in the room. Laura, your caseworker, will be up shortly to meet with you to go over your situation, needs, and further plans. Please note that anytime you leave the premises, you will need to turn the key in to me or whoever is sitting at the reception, okay?" LaShaun's eyes tried to meet his but he could not bring himself to make eye contact. Instead, his eyes focused on the room that had unfurled before him.

"Okay," Ralph managed to answer her. With that, she dangled the key in front of him for him to take. He gingerly took the key from her hand, walked inside the room, shut the door and just stared blankly at the wall.

A very pink wall.

In fact, the wall was so pink (how pink was it?), it reminded Ralph of the freshman psychology course he took in college that mentioned how Pepto-Bismol-pink was the color determined by most insane asylums and prisons to help in de-stressing and stabilizing psychiatric patients and convicted criminals. According to his professor at the time, pink is supposed to elicit feelings of tranquility, order, and peace. Oh, the irony of how that was exactly what Ralph needed right now although he didn't find the irony all that amusing.

The next thing he noted, other than the obtrusive pink-ness of the walls, was the twin-sized cot emblazoned with the Red Cross logo on it. In fact, it was the same blanket that Steve had handed him earlier in order to wipe him down from the sprinkler system. The blanket was neatly tucked in on all four corners—possibly military style—where a quarter would have bounced back up if dropped on it.

As he glanced across the room, he noticed that everything in the room was of military-order. The curtains looked freshly cleaned, starched and maybe even ironed and they, too, looked to be of the same material as the blanket. For sure, it was the same design. There was a white, shaggy throw rug on the floor next to the bed—thankfully it bared no logo or design and it matched the same bath mat that was next to the toilet in the tiny bathroom. He noticed the hotel-sized toiletries on the sink and shower stall. He was thankful that although this looked like a dorm room, there would be no need to share toilets and showers and used this as his first opportunity to relieve himself since his drunken stupor.

After flushing the toilet and opening an individually sized bar of soap with which he washed his hands, Ralph made his way over to the two-chaired dining table. Made of lacquered pinewood, the table really couldn't be called a dining room table since it could only accommodate food plates for one person, even though there were two chairs on either side of the table. Ralph slid one of the chairs out from underneath the table and slumped his body into it. He propped his head up with his right hand, right elbow leaning on the table and let out a heavy sigh.

He mentally played over the events from this morning from entering the office at seven am in order to catch Paris and Prague as they began their afternoon conference calls. He had a busy day blocked out—up until one pm, which was pretty typical for him. Since he was on this international project, most of his days were spent on early morning calls with Europe, the Middle East and Africa, and late night conversations with Asia and Australia. It seemed that the only time he had free over these last few months had been a few hours in the late afternoon where the only ones working were in the United States. Given he was not assigned to any projects overseeing US operations or finance, he used that time to get caught up on the dozens of emails he had been copied on or to run reports as was routinely requested from the regions. Occasionally, he would call Connie and Michael when his son would be getting home from school about this time.

It certainly was not enough time to travel back to the suburbs to see family when he was living at home and then get back to the office for the evening calls. Connie had asked him why he couldn't just work from home and take the calls from there. Ralph shook his head at Connie whenever this topic came up; some of the calls were video calls and he wanted to have the right ambience for the background—it was always best to appear fully professional for his offshore colleagues and that meant taking the call from the conference room or the board room. When PhasInt cleared out by five thirty, Ralph could have virtually any conference room and access to technology that he needed. He couldn't appear THAT professional and corporate if he were to take the call from home.

Ralph winced at the memory of the argument that drove him to move out over exactly this issue. "You're married to your job! Why don't you just buy a cot to put in your office and stay there?" Connie had angrily shouted at him through the phone when Ralph had to bow out at the last minute from attending Michael's move up ceremony from second grade. It wasn't something he had foreseen—the entire Korea team had asked him to help them with their budget setting sessions.

"If you really wanted to be here, you would have taken a vacation day," she stammered through what he knew were chokes and sobs of tears of anger and disappointment.

"Connie, you know that's not fair. It's just second grade." Ralph regretted the words as soon as they came out of his mouth.

"Forget it. Stay where you are. You obviously don't need us and given that we got through the day by ourselves, we don't need you either." With that, Connie hung up the phone. Ralph wanted to wait until she had calmed down to call her back but then he got to working on a report and started taking the calls and next thing he knew it was after ten pm.

Ralph texted her: “Late pm. Staying @ hotel. Call u 2moro.”

She didn’t return his text.

Chapter Five

The Case Worker

A knock came at his door.

"Mr. Pibbs?" he could barely hear through the door. That was actually a good sign as it meant he likely wouldn't be able to hear others walking through the hallways. Ralph had generally been a solidly sound sleeper until the last few months when calls, deadlines, projects, and family issues pervaded his thoughts and ebbed in and out of his dreams, causing him to wake up frequently at the slightest sound.

He stood up, walked to the door and opened it, "Yes?"

"Hi. I'm Laura Garcia, the caseworker who's been assigned to you. Do you mind if we go to one of the community rooms to talk?"

Ralph noticed a doe-like quality about Laura immediately. Of medium height and slender build, with what he imagined was long, dark hair that was folded neatly into a bun atop her head, she had expressive brown eyes and a fragile quality about her. This was amplified by the expression of expectancy and the deliberate way she moved her arms and stood in the hallway. She seemed graceful, like a ballerina. A ballerina wearing khaki pants and a beige, buttoned down blouse that revealed tiny, gold jewelry accents adorning her neck, ears, and wrists. Her petite, feminine features were without mascara or lipstick, and she looked natural with a healthy glow, not tired and washed out, as many women do without make up.

Ralph figured there wasn't enough room at his little table for them to talk so responded, "Sure," and snatched the room key from the table before exiting into the hallway. It was the only item now in his pocket and in his possession.

"Fantastic. We'll just head over to the community room on this floor if nobody is using it. Not only will it be more comfortable for us, but it provides safety for us to meet in a public place," Laura continued. Ralph reasoned that made sense as he followed her back toward the elevators to the end of the corridor and then to the right. At the intersection of corridors, a small room with card table, sofa and giant, flat-screen television greeted them. The walls were filled with tributes to Philadelphia firefighters who had made great sacrifices of health and even life during the call of duty.

"As you can see, this is our "Hero" room," explained Laura. Ralph could only nod. He had not yet made eye contact with her—similar to his treatment of LaShaun—and was curious to understand Laura's role.

"Why don't we have a seat at the table? I've got your intake documents as provided to me by Steve. Sounds like you've had quite an ordeal today," Laura posited.

"It's been pretty surreal," Ralph agreed as he pulled out and then sat in the rigid, plastic chair. Laura sat directly across from him and laid out a red folder in front of her. She started sorting through some of the documents, obviously looking for one item in particular. When she found it, she snatched it out of the folder and placed it in front of herself. She then produced a pen from her handbag.

"Well, I am here to help you during this time. According to the paperwork provided by Steve, a blaze went off in your apartment that has left you without a place to stay. The apartment has some smoke damage and some of your furnishings have been destroyed; your building management is doing a proper assessment and restoration of the facility which necessitates you be out of your home for the time being. I understand your wallet was included in the fire which prevents you from accessing any financial resources. Is that correct?" Laura asked.

"Yes, that's pretty much what happened," Ralph was thankful she did not mention how he was the cause for the blaze. Her tone was non-judgmental and matter-of-fact.

"It looks to me like you need some financial resources to get you through the next couple of days. Did you bring any clothes with you?"

"Just what I'm wearing although the receptionist—I forget her name—said there would be clothes for me in the basement?"

"Okay, we will need to get you a stipend to get some clothes over the weekend unless you think you can gain access to the clothes in your apartment. I wouldn't worry about the clothes in the basement—it's mostly unopened packages of socks and under garments. What about any medications you are taking that you need to refill? I want to be as complete as possible. It's a difficult time but you will get through this," she said with a smile. For the first time, Ralph looked at her intently in the face.

He was grateful for her compassion and positivity. Regarding her question on medications, that was a good one. The short answer was 'no' but that's only because he hadn't been taking his Pantoprazole to treat his GERD on a regular basis. More often than not, since he did not like labeling himself as being 'on prescription meds' even if he needed to be, he would routinely pop a TUMS whenever his acid reflux would appear. He could probably pick up some Prilosec OTC at a CVS. If he had money. Which, at this point he didn't and his stomach had been in knots since this morning's events.

"I'm supposed to be taking something daily but I haven't been taking it regularly so I guess the answer is technically yes since I'll likely need it this weekend. Um, let me see what I'm doing about my cash situation before I respond on the underwear." He was pretty grossed out at the idea, actually, even though she did say it was 'unopened packaging.' Yuck.

"All right, I'll add that in too. All your meals will be covered by the Red Cross House so there is no need for funds for food." Laura looked over her forms.

"Add what in? To what?"

"The Red Cross will issue you a debit card to help you with some of the losses you've just incurred in order to get you back on your feet."

"Really? I had no idea the Red Cross did that. I thought they just passed out blankets and cocoa and stuff during hurricanes and floods."

"Oh no, Mr. Pibbs. We aim to help you get back on your feet in as little time necessary. Let me go over this form with you," Laura finished filling in a few areas on the forms before passing the various sheets of paper over to Ralph.

Laura pointed to a few lines here and there on the sheet while explaining, "This amount is to be used as a clothing allowance. And, this amount is to be used for the restoration of your pharmaceuticals. You'll have seven days in which to use this card otherwise all funds will revert back to the Red Cross. You'll need to follow the instructions on this sheet," as she pointed to another sheet of paper, "by setting up a PIN and so forth before you can use it. I strongly advise you do that as soon as possible."

Ralph was impressed with the positivity in Laura's voice and the amazing services she was unfolding before him. He really had no idea a national—heck, international--organization did this? It was like being given free cash! He imagined that the accounting of it all must incredibly sophisticated and complicated. He gave silent props to the big organization helping out the little guy.

His thoughts returned to his immediate situation. "Speaking of using a phone to set up this card, I need to call my credit card companies and banks and such to have them send me out new cards. I will also need to get a new license for proof of ID. I have so much to do right now."

"No problem. There's a computer room downstairs that has a pay phone in it that you can use. Once you sign these forms, I can give you the tour of the facilities so you'll know where everything is. I have written you down for staying with us through the weekend with maybe an extension into the week, depending upon how the restoration in your apartment is coming along," Laura shoved a pen at Ralph, indicating the exact lines and pages on which he should sign his name.

"Thanks. This is a huge help. It's just…" Ralph trailed off.

"What?"

"Nothing. It's just, you're very nice, that's all."

"That's very nice of you to say. I love to help people. And, you'll meet lots of people here who are absolutely, positively dedicated to ensuring your health, safety and well-being. Things will get better. I see miracles happen every day. You will be back to your normal life in no time."

"I very much doubt that. I got fired today. That's what actually started the fire," he noted the irony of the use of terminology of fire at work versus fire at home. Both have the propensity to destroy lives, dreams, and hope.

"I'm so sorry to hear that. I know you don't need to hear platitudes right now but this just might be the best thing for you."

"That's preposterous! How can you say that?" Ralph almost exploded on her. He got to his feet wanting to get to that computer room so he could get started on his various calls and away from her Pollyanna attitude.

"I'm so sorry, Mr. Pibbs. I didn't mean to sound trite or

condescending. But, I've been where you are and I can now say that it's the best thing that happened to me. I mean, I've been fired, too," Laura seemed to back down a bit but still maintained her enthusiastic positivity. She got up to follow his lead, acknowledging that her paperwork and conversation pertaining to it were over. "Here, why don't we start making our way to the computer room?"

Ralph dutifully followed her out of the room, still smarting from her ignorance. He changed the subject away from him and back on her. "It looks like you've found yourself a good job".

Be Open To New Directions

"Indeed! Admittedly, I didn't think it was a good experience at all while I was terminated and then in transition. In fact, I was pretty negative about it given how I had dedicated my entire career to that company and how it all ultimately ended in demise. But, it gave me the time to reflect on my passions and values and now I'm doing what I love!" A broad smile beamed across her face.

"Where else were you a social worker?" Ralph inquired as they slowly made their way out of the tribute room toward the elevator.

"I wasn't a social worker before. I was in HR for a large, domestic retailer."

"Oh," Ralph just assumed this had been her line of work before. Ralph tried to place her age. Early thirties? She couldn't have worked someplace else for too long.

Laura trailed on through Ralph's expression. "I oversaw domestic recruiting for a major fashion chain in the mid-west that employed over ten thousand individuals—mostly part-timers although we did have full time management and scads of employees at corporate, particularly in marketing, merchandising and purchasing. I loved my job—interacting with people, helping them realize their professional goals as well as being an integral part of the management team dedicated completely to customer service. I got to develop training plans for literally thousands of people at one time. It was a fun experience."

The elevator arrived, they both stepped in and Laura pressed "B".

"Sounds like a very gratifying line of work," Ralph briefly and mentally reflected how people development had been one of his favorite activities as a manager, too. That is, when he had a team reporting to him.

Laura continued as the elevator slowly chugged its hydraulics down to the basement floor. "Well, a few years back we hit a major slump. Sales were off by double digits and we ended up closing almost twenty percent of our stores. Part time workers are used to the instability of layoffs and seasonal shopping patterns but when I had to go in and tell everyone that within three to six months they wouldn't have a job at all, it became very stressful."

By now, they'd made their way down to the basement area. They walked out of the elevator, took a left and Laura continued speaking as they walked down a darkened corridor.

"So, I became a 'reduction in workforce' expert tasked with creating, drafting, and communicating mass-scale closures around the country. I traveled to thirty-something states for a solid fourteen months, ensuring that the President's plan of reducing capital and personnel expenses was achieved in the timeframe he wanted in order to meet shareholder expectations. It wasn't the feel-good recruiting strategy any longer but a strategy of survival…and professional death for thousands. Because I was on the road so much, I missed a lot of HQ-based meetings to which I was never sent the Cliff-notes, although updates on my progress were needed prior to every call and meeting. Looking back, I can now see the positive in having me craft this impactful message to so many as I tried to do it with empathy and positivity. Personally, I'm thankful that I got through fourteen months as the closure plan was to last for another two months after that."

She paused and looked at Ralph to see if he was still paying attention. His eyes met hers and he lifted his eyebrows as if to prod her to continue.

"I had actually seen an email I probably wasn't supposed to see. An email had come in from a recruiter to our legal department and attached was a contract to hire an agency to do HR recruiting. I was a bit perplexed by this so I confronted my boss in person. I asked him about the email from this agency and he played all coy like he had no idea what I was talking about. He responded, 'How could we be hiring an outside agency to recruit when we are in a downsize mode?' and I accepted his answer at that. But, the fact of the matter is that any outside agency would have had to come through me and I sort of pushed aside the notion that I could or would be replaced. I mean, I had great confidence in my abilities and talents and never contemplated that my superior would actually get rid of me. I'd been a stellar performer."

Laura took in a deep breath as if to pause for artistic effect and slowed her footsteps to a snail's pace. She then continued her story.

"Then, after returning home from Dallas one Thursday afternoon a few weeks later, my boss asked me to meet him in the conference room for a 'debrief'. I walked into the conference room with my notebook from my recent trip to communicate the closure of stores throughout Texas and I noticed that he had the exact same 'pitch book' on the table that I had written and used when I was sharing the closure news with the employees. I guessed maybe it was an updated version he wanted to go over with me when I share the news with the employees in the field."

She paused and looked away.

"But, no. He read from my playbook word for word of the dialogue I'd written for the closed-store employees. He was using MY pitch on ME."

That's cold, was all Ralph could think to himself. What a bastard. No, what a lying, lazy bastard!

"It was clearly ridiculous as he was very uncomfortable with the wording meant for lower level employees of a different circumstance. Although his hands were trembling and he couldn't look me in the eye, it was a pretty straightforward conversation. That was it; I left. I had been in this situation on the other end, obviously, and you don't want to get into the details and particulars with any employee about what went wrong, who was at fault, or what the state of the business was. None of this was personal. I knew all of that. Like I said, I had written the book on it. My boss gave me my severance agreement and that was it. I was just mortified and wanted to leave immediately thereafter—no need to hang around and tell my colleagues I'd just gotten let go."

Ralph definitely understood that sentiment. Then again, he wasn't really given a choice of hanging around and saying goodbye to anyone. No farewell party, no goodbye luncheon. No, he was escorted out like a criminal who had misappropriated funds or stolen company property. He wasn't sure if it was a good thing to know that someone else had felt the sting of termination.

Laura stopped walking altogether and changed topic. "Let me show you this room, really quickly, before we get to the computer room. It will only take a second and I want you to see it," Laura interrupted the playback of her story which Ralph was now very interested to hear the rest of. "This is our storage room" and with that, she quickly punched in a code on the door handle lock that popped open the heavy, metal door.

Ralph thought it looked, upon first glance, like a dog kennel. Chain link fence from floor to ceiling. Neatly laid out cells that looked very similar to the indoor doggy runs he'd seen when he got his first dog from a local animal orphanage only, there was no stench of animal urine or feces (although there was a slightly stale smell of smoke that seemed to waft around his nostrils).

A few of the compartments had boxes in them. One had a suitcase. One had a lonely kid's training bicycle. Another was filled to the brim with kids' toys, a basketball hoop, and a massive dollhouse. Most of the compartments, however, were totally empty.

"This is our storage room for our guests who stay in the House. Every guest is allotted a compartment where they can store their salvaged items from their home. Your compartment, Mr. Pibbs, is number twenty five," as she motioned to an empty unit at the far end of the right side of the room.

Ralph wondered why she was showing him this room since he obviously had nothing to store. It was almost like she was rubbing his nose in his loss and the losses of others given that more than half of the storage units were without any material possession contained therein.

Again, as if on cue, Laura responded, "I think it's important for people to know that one, we have planned a place for them to guard their remaining mementos and household items but two—and most importantly—you will come to realize that your life is not measured by your possessions."

Her positivity astounded him. As he looked around again at the earthly leftovers of the other guests staying at the House, he internally questioned how many of them felt as positive about their experience as Laura does?

Laura turned to head back towards the door.

Ralph followed her in silence.

They both stepped through the door which Laura locked behind her. She motioned gracefully with her right arm to continue walking down the hallway to the computer room.

"I'm sure you are wondering how I can say all of this. While I didn't suffer a fire and lose most of my possessions, I did lose my self-respect and confidence. I lost all of the people that I believed were friends at work. It turns out that they were only work friends—a big difference. And, I certainly lost my livelihood. Being single at the time, I didn't have anyone to pay my bills for me and I fell into a deep depression immediately following my termination. I couldn't believe the way I was treated—so cold and impersonally. I felt so humiliated. I was so angry. Ashamed. Embarrassed. I didn't start looking for a job immediately and basically became a hermit. I'd say I was in a state of 'learned helplessness'—a place where I'd come not to rely on myself anymore and I stopped believing in myself. I lost…my freedom. I lost…my identity."

They arrived at another door with a narrow, vertical windowpane that demonstrated that this room was clearly the computer room, judging by the elongated desk with several older-model computers symmetrically spaced upon it. Ralph waited for Laura to open the door before going in.

"I had been exposed to so many wonderful experiences in my career and from a strategic perspective, I had always been involved in the conversations that needed to be had on a local level. And, while I tried to be open and transparent in my communications with the thousands of employees I met, I am sad to say that I was not given the same respect. I think the senior management team owed it to me to discuss the changes that were being planned at my level, just as I had done with employees at the store level. I felt that if a company esteems their people, it should have an open and honest conversation that would demonstrate trust in one another that fostered mutual respect. I didn't get that and it was quite a bitter pill to swallow,"

Laura clasped the door handle in her hands and twisted it.

"I'm sorry. I shouldn't burden you with my story," Laura proceeded, gently opening the door and motioning for Ralph to enter.

"Actually, I want to hear how this ends and how you landed here. If you were in charge of the teams recruiting for tens of thousands of temporary and part time workers, this must be quite a decrease in responsibility for you. Not to mention pay."

They both entered the computer room where Laura continued. "I'll make this quick as I know you need to get on the horn to start calling places and activating your new card from us. Well, the short of it is that I did some soul searching to get to the heart of what I really loved and wanted to do."

"Your passion?" Ralph chimed in, thinking of how Steve was so emphatic about following his passion.

"Exactly! I am passionate about helping others. I took a few online tests, and was invited to participate in a local roundtable with other HR colleagues I'd met through various HR associations whom I greatly respected. All of the emotional trauma I was going through and wallowing in self-pity was totally draining me. Like I said, I was incredibly bitter for months following my termination and depression seemed to keep me in bed most days (which is probably why I didn't find a job right away). One of my friends forced me to go to a party just to get out of the house and everyone I met kept asking me if I was married? No. Did I have kids? No. What did I do for a living? I couldn't give an affirmative response to any of them. I came home disgusted, depressed and resolved I'd never go out again. What did I have to live for?

"But, I kept meeting voluntarily with some women who I'd met through the various HR conferences I'd attended over the years. They seemed to want to invest in me and little by little, I started trusting them with confidential information about myself, my values, and my goals and with that, I started trusting myself again. I wrote my goals, skills, and values down and compared one list against the others. Then, when I started thinking about options and possible next steps, I could honestly ask myself, 'did this fit?' and if the answer was "No", have the courage to determine that I would be more happy in an environment where I was hands on and helping people through personal crisis situations. I certainly could relate with that! I determined I needed to go back to school to get my Masters of Social Work so I could be a bona fide social worker. I wanted to get out of corporate America since our values didn't match."

"That must have taken a long time or did you have a coach, too?" Ralph mentally referenced back to Steve, again.

"Other than that weekly group of women, no. From my years in helping employees, I already had a solid idea of what color was my parachute, to paraphrase it. But, I needed to look at my career from a different angle and be open to a new direction, if warranted, including title, pay and work environment. Those ladies helped me see that; they definitely made me uncomfortable with their questions but they were what I needed at the time. And, quite frankly, with as negative as I was during those months and even years since the separation, I would not have been a good interview candidate anyway. Negativity doesn't show up well in an interview or office, even if camouflaged in a nice suit."

Stay Away From Negativity

Ralph winced at her words, peering down at his own rumpled suit that he'd been in since early morning.

Laura continued, "Negativity will just kill you from the inside out and the only person you are hurting is yourself. I had to remove myself from negative people—since I was one at the time—and I didn't want to be further influenced by those who were dour, hopeless, and discouraging. So, I put my time into studying and helping others knowing that something good would come of it in the end. And it has!"

The gums of her teeth were totally exposed by her massive grin. The pearly whites weren't so pearly white—more like the color of white corn and similar in size. The niblets were totally straight on top and slightly crooked on the bottom giving Ralph the impression her parents could only afford braces for one side of her mouth when she was a child. Her gumminess gave way to a gentility that made her approachable and warm. Human.

"How did you get out of that negativity? It seems it could have enveloped you?"

"Great question. Like I said, I had a great support group of ladies. Some I had known for a while and some who were less than casual acquaintances. One of them brought a Dale Carnegie lecture series for us to listen to entitled, 'How to win friends and influence people'. She would then email us a photo of 'Act enthusiastic, BE enthusiastic' which re-emphasized being positive, even if you have to fake it. There is a certain authenticity to the adage, 'Fake it 'til you make it'. It's certainly true with attitude."

Ralph thought Laura must have bought into the new age, hipster, and hype.

"Had I not been fired and forced to re-evaluate my priorities and passions, I would not have gone to grad school. Had I not gone to grad school, I would not have met my husband and his kids. He was there doing an Executive MBA and was recently divorced; he wanted to put his anger regarding his divorce to good use too. We were quite the irate pair when we first met! Hah! So, when he got a job in Philly a few years ago after we both graduated, I came across this opportunity. I've been here ever since. I would have never desired to go back to school at 38 but I would not have done it had I not been forced to do it," Laura beamed.

Thirty-eight, pondered Ralph. That puts her in her early forties now. She was apparently well preserved judging by her scarcity of wrinkles, gray hair or sagging skin—all of which he had in abundance, and, he was in his early forties, too.

"It's obvious you love what you do and you're good at it." Ralph meant what he said.

"Why, thank you. Well, I will leave you alone for now but I will be checking in on you throughout your stay this weekend to make sure everything is moving in the right direction. Remember, stay positive and keep yourself open to new possibilities," she daintily extended her hand to him.

Ralph took her bony hand in his and shook it lightly. "Thank you for your help. And, your advice."

"It's my pleasure. Oh! I forgot to mention that dinner is served until 6:30pm. It's already after five so just make a mental note so you don't miss out on the meal. Mel does a great job and you won't go hungry here! The cafeteria is on the first floor. Remember where the reception is? Well, instead of heading to the elevator and your room on the left, go down the opposite corridor to the right. It's straight ahead and you can't miss it. Bon appetite!"

With that, Laura flashed another gummy grin, waved her slender fingers in the air like a dance team member doing a jazz hand, and disappeared through the computer room door.

Chapter Six

The Computer Room

Ralph got busy on his calls by first researching the websites of the credit card companies to find their toll free numbers. He determined which one of the six computers looked to be the most familiar to him in order to search for his credit card issuing company as well as his bank, credit union, and Starwood Hotels loyalty program. He did not intend to stay longer at the Red Cross House than he had to. Not that there was anything wrong with it, it just wasn't his, um, style. He wondered if the House offered maid service in the morning and turn down service at night? Probably not.

He opened up Internet Explorer as that was the only icon on the desktop of the computer other than the trash can and he busily started entering information. He and Connie had been quite fastidious about their expenses over the years and had kept their cards to a minimum. He routinely used a Corporate American Express card for business expenses and only had two personal credit cards for his personal use. He couldn't fully remember if they were both issued by Citibank or one from HSBC. Or was that his debit card? Connie really kept up with the personal finance part of things given that the majority of Ralph's expenses were work related. He looked up the numbers for both companies, just to be on the safe side.

He was glad to have had the red folder and pen that Laura had given to him in the upstairs community room so he could write down on the back of the folder the phone numbers for each company for when he called them. It didn't make sense to him to research one company first, make a call, and return to the computer to research the next company. It wasn't efficient and if Ralph was good at analytics and reports, he was phenomenal at efficiency.

For those programs where he didn't know his number, Ralph logged into one of his two personal email accounts. One was kept just for work related personal emails in case he was working from home or traveling and couldn't gain access to PhasInt's network and the other was strictly personal for use in corresponding with old friends, which he was lousy at and always relegated to Connie. He was organized enough to have kept every single welcome email received from the various companies and organizations he belonged to. In fact, he had all of the emails ever sent to him dating back to 2001 when he first opened up his personal Yahoo! account, whether an announcement for the latest musical release for a certain artist, to neighborhood town watch updates, to coupons for his favorite Mexican restaurant, to receipts for all of his travel invoices for easier expense report accounting.

He'd get peeved when Connie would go through his emails to 'clean them up' as he liked everything as he left it. She hadn't gone through his emails since he moved out and his inbox had grown to well over 3200 emails—most of them unread and unopened. Lord knows what kinds of emails were in there now.

Ralph inhaled a deep breath. He needed the oxygen as he felt he'd been running on adrenaline since noon. Actually, he needed either a cup of coffee to keep going right now or a good night's sleep that would last until Monday when his cards arrived.

Almost done, he thought. After exhausting his mental Rolodex of companies and organizations he needed to call in order to resume some normalcy to his life, Ralph logged out of his various open windows.

For the first time since Laura gave him the folder, Ralph looked though all of the documents in the red binder. In it contained a write up of his incident as written by Steve, the financial calculation worksheet as written up by Laura, instructions for activating his temporary debit card, a code of acceptable behavior and rules for the House, the most recent quarterly newsletter from the Red Cross, and a few sheets of blank paper. Had he seen them earlier, he could have written his notes down on them. No use in crying over very small amounts of spilled milk. Larger cows needed to be milked now!

Ralph dragged his metal chair with lumpy-cushion seat over to the pay phone and began the process of calling his creditors using the 1-800 access numbers he'd researched. Even though he was Platinum Elite for many of his cards, he did not find the toll free numbers for his particular brands and was relegated to dialing the customer service numbers used for the general public.

He hadn't used a pay phone in years and certainly didn't have the change to make direct-dial calls. He started with the most important one that he would need come morning, his Visa card.

A usual, automated message directed him to enter in his 16-digit credit card number. He didn't have it and although he was a numbers guy, he did not have this or any of his card numbers committed to memory. He pressed '0' for operator to bypass the automated system and waited a few moments for the call to go through.

Another recorded message came on asking him what his call was regarding. Ralph punched '0' again and hoped it would get him through. He hated these recordings although, from a business perspective, he certainly appreciated their time and money-savings propositions. He just didn't have the time or attitude to want to deal with them right now. He needed a live person. Almost three hours had already elapsed from the time his apartment caught fire and wiped out his personal identity and access to cash.

Another recorded message prompted him to enter in his sixteen-digit credit card number. Ralph pressed "0" again and waited.

"I'm sorry; your number was not recognized. Please wait," said the recorded voice. "The average wait time for this call is seven minutes. You are number seven in queue."

Seriously? Ralph tilted his head back and heard the crinkles pop. It felt good, in a painful sort of way. Since he had seven minutes to wait, he put the phone receiver atop the pay phone unit and swung his head from side to side, slowly feeling the muscles give way to the pressure in his neck. He lifted his arms toward the ceiling then pulled them back behind his neck and flexed. He could no longer hear the music coming through the phone and picked up the receiver quickly.

"Thank you for calling Visa. My name is Stacy and I am proudly based in the US. How may I assist you today?"

"Hi. This is Ralph Pibbs. I'm calling to report a lost card." He wasn't really sure if being burned in a booze-induced blaze counted as 'lost' but he didn't need to go into the details.

"Certainly sir. I'll need the card number please."

"I don't have it. It's lost. Can I give you my social security number and password?"

"Yes, that will work."

After exchanging the basic information that confirmed Ralph's identity, Stacy, the customer service representative, informed Ralph that the shipment would be sent out on Saturday for Monday arrival to his home since they'd already missed the pick-up cut-off for the day.

Ralph had never bothered to change over his address to the apartment, knowing that Connie always reconciled the home finances with the card charges. He also believed that his move to the city would just be a temporary stay while he and Connie worked things out. Besides, with seeing Michael every other weekend, Connie handed him his mail in a grocery bag along with any UPS deliveries that came delivered to his attention—usually his monthly installment of his Cigar-of-the-Month club.

If the replacement card was sent to Connie, she'd ask about why he lost his card in the first place and he didn't want to get into that with her just yet. Plus, he didn't have the keys to his car in order to drive out there to pick up the delivery.

"Please send it to my new address in Philadelphia," Ralph interjected.

"I'm sorry sir, but I am unable to do that for you. For security purposes, I must send it to the address we have on file."

"That's stupid. What if I'm on vacation and not at my house? Let me speak with a supervisor," Ralph didn't have time for this time-wasting nonsense. He needed to speak with someone who could make action happen. He heard a click and was immediately placed into customer service hell, or Muzak. Ralph noted that the music being played, a version of classical guitar, might not be so bad if it didn't sound so muffled or muted.

His mind quickly fluttered over to Spain, where he and Connie spent their honeymoon. Since she wasn't able to finish up her college degree in international relations, Ralph thought the least he could do was take her to where she'd always wanted to go: the royal palace of Aranjuez, the Alhambra in Granada, and Seville.

They started their journey in Madrid where they ate paella on their first night and attended a flamenco show. Connie was zealous to practice her Spanish learned in high school and college. Even Ralph knew that she badly mangled some words and had an atrocious American accent, but the locals appreciated her enthusiasm and desire to speak the language. Ralph did get a little embarrassed for her when she misused the word 'embarazada' to describe her embarrassment over her mispronunciations. Even he knew that meant 'pregnant' and not 'embarrassed', as she'd intended. Everyone seemed to have a good-natured laugh over it.

Regardless, Connie's affinity towards Spain and the Spanish culture stemmed back to childhood when her father urged her to take up guitar lessons. He meant electric guitar and rock n roll but she chose the classical route and tried to practice at least once a week. She said it eased her nerves and gave her something lovely to think on and look forward to each week. Wanting to do something equally as lovely for her while they were newly dating, Ralph made a point to get tickets to see the famous Romero Brothers when they had passed through their college town on a nationwide tour of college campuses.

Ralph deemed they were nothing spectacular. Connie loved them. He bought her Andres Segovia and Christopher Parkening CDs for Christmas that year—he liked them much better than the troubadours. In fact, he used the music of Parkening's "Jubilation" CD as the background setting for his proposal to her later that year.

"Hello, Mr. Pibbs? My name is Bruce. May I get your card number, please?" a male voice came over the phone.

"Did the girl not tell you what I needed?"

"Unfortunately not as the call was transferred to me directly from our main call center. Would you mind starting off with your card number? "

"What kind of crap service is this? I don't have the number. I had the last girl look it up using my social security number, address and answers to security questions. " The frustration was starting to mount and he could feel himself losing control of his temper.

"I'm sorry for the confusion, sir. Let's get this sorted for you right away. Let's start with your information again."

Ralph relayed the same information he'd just given to Stacy. This time, he added a dose of exasperation to his intonation and inflection.

"So, if I'm understanding you correctly, you need us to send a replacement card out. Is that correct?"

"Sort of. I need the replacement sent to a place other than my home address."

"That's outside of our policy, sir…" Bruce was cut off.

Ralph didn't give Bruce the opportunity to say anything past that. "You call this customer-freakin'-service? I am in a pinch and I need you to send me my replacement card on the next FedEx flight out to the address I designate. I will give you whatever piece of information to prove my identity to you but I need this done now and if you can't do it, I want to speak to your manager and if he can't do it I want to speak to HIS boss! Is that understood?"

"Yes, sir. Had you let me finish, I would have shared with you that I will need to get further information from you to ensure the fullest security on your account. I am sure you can appreciate our attention to your current needs as well as your privacy and data security needs. Let me just go through some items with you," Bruce kept an even tone throughout.

Ralph looked around the room to ensure no one else was hiding in a corner, near the bookshelves, or under a desk. He hadn't noticed anyone coming in but he certainly did not want to be giving out private financial information within earshot of a soul. Ralph then began answering Bruce's mandatory identification questions and directed him to send the replacement card to his apartment. He figured if it could not be sent out until a Monday delivery, he would absolutely, positively be back in his apartment by then. Bruce obtained Ralph's current address, exchanged some final pleasantries, and terminated the call after giving Ralph the FedEx shipment tracking number.

Ralph exhaled as he hung up the phone and hoped the rest of the calls were less taxing on his nerves. While he ultimately will get his card—on Monday—he wasn't pleased about the runaround it took to get him what he wanted. Upon reflection, he wasn't too pleased with his negativity, anger and frustration that bubbled up into the call.

Laura had just cautioned him about negativity and being open to new directions. He was sure she wasn't talking about interactions with incompetent customer service idiots. Or, was she speaking about a way of life in being positive and open minded in aspects including, but not limited to, his professional career?

He took out a sheet of blank paper and wrote:

- STAY AWAY FROM NEGATIVITY
- BE OPEN TO NEW DIRECTIONS

Ralph felt that was a good idea. It would help him retain a semblance of the control he had lost almost six hours ago. If he wasn't in control of his attitude and actions, what was he in control of? Pretty much nothing.

Ralph resumed calls of the dozen or so companies he needed to call over the next hour and a half in order to receive new cards and update credit information.

In between calls, Ralph pondered his current situation and reflected on the passion with which both Steve and Laura took to their roles. He thought back to what he loved about his job. Was it running complex spreadsheets that highlighted his analytical mastery? Truth be told, no.

Lately, that's what he'd become, though, is a glorified report maker who not only took orders of and designed complex reports for various regions around the world, but he also articulated the value of said reports back to the teams and how to utilize them to maximize commercial relationships and lower SG&A costs. He was fond of the advisory role he'd recently taken up although, if he were really honest with himself, he craved the leadership positions with which he'd been entrusted in the past. Leading his teams with inspiring messages, crafting and articulating a vision, and supplying his teams with the tools they needed to achieve it were key motivators for himself.

In thinking back on how both Steve and Laura had uncovered their passions, they had worked with an outplacement firm, coach, or networked with peers at various functional associations and industry-based conferences.

Had he been doing any of that lately?

No.

But, how could he? Most of his allies at work had moved on to other companies or he had surpassed them in his ascent through various departments and levels. He lost touch with practically all of them. As an indicator of how Connie kept in contact with all of his friends at home, he did not have a 'Connie' at work who would be the relationship master he needed. Also, most honestly, he had not given much effort in his career to official mentors or official networking with professional trade and industry associations because he was simply way too busy. Between the demands of a global career and the needs of a young family sandwiched in between travel to branch locations and a stint overseas, Ralph had no time or inclination for unnecessary and frivolous extra-curricular activities.

The quality of Ralph's work was flawless—all of his performance reviews said so. So, how did he end up unemployed after doing everything right, working his tail off, and sacrificing so much of his personal time? He wasn't sure. But, he was committed to finding out not only why, but what he could do to get out of this situation.

He pulled out Steve's business card and rewrote Steve's scribbles from the back of his card on to the sheet of paper that contained

Laura's advice:

- PURSUE YOUR PASSION
- ENGAGE A TRUSTED BUSINESS ADVISOR, COACH, OR RESPECTED ALLY

He was beginning to see a pattern here of how these suggestions had not only helped two people in bizarrely similar situations at one point in their lives but also could impact Ralph.

Chapter Seven

Play Time

The door to the computer room jostled with a bit of a struggle. Apparently, the person on the outside of the room was having difficulty in maneuvering the heavy, wooden door. Ralph placed his notes in his folder, laid them in front of a computer, and walked to the door.

Through the slivered window in the door, he saw the little girl in purple attempting to pull the door open with all her might. Ralph helped her by turning the knob to disengage the latch and the door swung open into the little girl, nearly knocking her to the floor. She ran past Ralph to one of the six computers at the rectangular wooden table and picked up the mouse. Ralph looked at her as she breezed by him and then looked back at the door. Her mother was approaching from down the hallway.

“Ramona! Do NOT get on that computer until I get there!” The mom swiftly approached Ralph. “Thank you for opening the door. Pardon me, I have a little girl with ants-in-her-pants who wants to play her game.”

“Mommy, c’mere! Log me on, now! Please?”

“Did you say ‘thank you’ to the nice man for opening up the door for you?”

Ramona nodded her head to indicate yes and stood in front of one of the aged computers. Ralph didn’t recall the little girl saying anything to him but with some kids these days, he didn’t expect too much.

“Ramona, did you ask the man if he was using any of these computers?”

“Mom-mee! The computers are empty!” Ramona let out exasperatedly. She clearly was not into taking any time away from her favorite computer game. Her mom had promised her she could have fifteen minutes of computer time after dinner and she had no desire to involve a strange man in this process.

Her mom wasn't having any of Ramona's rudeness and rebutted, "Ramona Raquel. You will look at me when I am speaking with you. Ramona?"

Ramona looked up at her mom with big brown eyes and eyelashes that seemed to extend until Tuesday. "Mommy, please? Can I play?"

The mom turned to Ralph and apologized for her daughter's behavior. "You know how kids are with computers these days. Are you using any of these computers?"

"No. Go right ahead," Ralph responded. He smiled at the lady. In contrast to her daughter, she was not wearing anything quite so colorful or frilly. She looked quite plain, tired, and pretty typical for a mother of an active young child. He guessed Ramona was maybe five or six and the mother in her late twenties. Mom was casually attired in blue jeans and a worn, yellow t-shirt emblazoned with the words "Woman of Faith" in fancy cursive writing. The collar of the shirt was bedecked with beads and glitter, some of them missing in certain parts along her neckline.

Ralph watched as mom logged on to the computer closest to the door and typed in the web address for Nick Junior. Ralph was pretty familiar with that link given that it was the same one on which he and Michael would play games. Ralph preferred the video games to the physically demanding ones like baseball; at least here he didn't have to break a sweat although sometimes his fingers didn't fully cooperate with the games. He was also embarrassed when he didn't know the answers to some of the trivia games they played. Apparently he wasn't smarter than a fifth grader; he wasn't even smarter than a first grader oftentimes. Michael always won whether Ralph wanted to let him or not.

The mom brought up the site to "Bubble Puppy Treat Pop Game". It was not one familiar to Ralph; Michael seemed to prefer the ones with UmiZoomi. He was particularly fascinated by the space people and their ability to fly everywhere. This one looked to be about cute little dogs eating treats. He couldn't help himself but watch and caught himself staring at the banter between mother and daughter. Mom caught his glance.

"I'm sorry for staring. My son likes to play on Nick Junior, too," Ralph interrupted mom and daughter play time.

"Oh. Yes. It's very fun and educational. I only allow her a few minutes every day though. She tries to push the limits of time and my patience sometimes. You know how kids are, they want to do everything on their own," she giggled, and turned around and away from the computer to screen to flash a welcoming smile at him.

"Mommy. I don't want you to play with me today. I just want to play by myself." Ramona sure is a pistol, judged Ralph, the corners of his lips turning upwards in amusement.

"Of course, baby." Mom turned to Ralph. "It's none of my business but what brought you to the House?"

Ralph certainly didn't want to get into the details with her although she obviously was under the same distressing and disturbing situation if she was a tenant like he. He responded a curt, "Apartment fire. And you?" He wanted to quickly get the focus off of him.

"Same thing. Did your landlord help you out at all?"

"I don't know if I follow you. What do you mean, help me out?" Ralph asked.

"Well, our fire started as an electrical fire. Seems that there was faulty wiring. It actually started in our bedroom. My boyfriend and I were asleep. Our dog woke us up barking because he smelled the smoke.

Unfortunately, since the fire was contained within the walls of our closet, the first things to go up were all our clothes and then it just spread like wildfire throughout the house. It was just devastating," the mom had a far off look in her eyes as if being present at the fire scene again.

"My first action was to get Ramona and her sister out of their room. My boyfriend called 911 immediately and me and the girls ran outside to knock on the neighbor's house for help. The girls were so scared. I didn't even realize we were all just in t-shirts and our underwear but I was so frightened that I didn't have time to look for anything for us to wear. I was terrified something happened to James since he was still in the building by the time we ran outside…" she trailed off.

"Mommy, look! I just scored the bonus bones!" Ramona butted in, totally oblivious to her mom's ongoing conversation with Ralph.

"That's great honey. Keep it going," the mom countered without missing a beat, her eyes firmly fixed on Ralph's.

"I'm so sorry for your ordeal," was all Ralph could say. He really didn't want to hear any more details but the mom pressed on.

"I didn't think I would see him again. The blaze from our closet was so hot and glowing. It nearly burst through the closet door and it had already started working its way on the carpet to the bed. Our little Malti-poo, Cinnamon, had jumped up on the bed and honestly, I wasn't even thinking about him—I needed to get to the girls quickly. I assumed James would have gotten him. The firemen said he was totally charred atop of the bed," she broke out into choked sobs and covered her face in her hands.

She whispered, "I'm sorry. I can't have Ramona see me like this or hear about Cinnamon. She doesn't know all the details. All we told the girls is that Cinnamon decided to stay with the firemen since they didn't have a dog for their truck. Ramona bought it but I think

Raluca is a little older and wiser. I've been talking with the social worker everyday but I'm still so sad about our little Cinnamon. The clothes and toys and furniture can all be replaced but, oh, I miss that fluffy little ball of fuzz."

Ralph didn't know what to say. He was never an animal person and didn't really understand people who were. He managed an, "I'm so sorry for your loss." He was actually quite uncomfortable with the conversation and not sure how to contribute.

"Thank you. Like I said, me, the girls and James finally made it out. We woke up our entire block with all our screaming. Seems that the fire had spread to our neighbor's houses too. One of them was abandoned and had squatters in it. I think they were feeding off our electricity wires. The firemen said that was a possibility and the electrical fire was totally preventable. Who knows who else in the city has rigged wires like we did? According to the firemen, it happens quite a bit in the city. I never gave a thought to anything like that—ever! Our landlord denied everything and blamed everything on us! Can you imagine?"

She gave Ralph no time to answer but just continued, "I have been really angry with our landlord for putting us into that type of environment but we just didn't know. At least the people here have been really good to us and as you can see, the fire hasn't seemed to bother the girls," the mom pointed to her daughter.

"Where is your other daughter?" Ralph politely inquired really not wanting to know more but feeling that this woman's confession was rather cathartic for him, as it was for her.

"She's with a friend for the weekend. She's a little older than Ramona and since we've been here for three weeks already, she wanted to spend time at 'a real house' as she said. So, it's just me and Ramona tonight. James works the second shift as a security guard for one of the buildings downtown so he won't get in 'til after midnight.

Thankfully, he has been able to keep his schedule and his job throughout all this. Unfortunately, I had to quit mine to keep up with all the paperwork, ensure the girls started school on time and look for a new place to live. It's not been easy," the mom looked at Ralph.

"Mommy! Look! I'm already at level six!" Ramona squealed with delight.

"Good job honey. Let's see if you can get up to level ten in record time," the mom shot back.

"No, I see it hasn't. I didn't realize you could stay here for that long?" Ralph hadn't really considered how long families could stay at the House. He was intending to be out in three days. He assumed most people here would want to do the same.

"We are actually coming up on the time limit but I am so thankful that we have had this calm oasis in the middle of this storm. You never think that something like this is going to happen to you and then one day your entire life is turned around. I am eternally grateful that there are groups out there that can help us and provide resources for us. I would have never known what my first step would be but when my caseworker handed me that debit card filled with funds to replace our clothes and other necessary items, hoo boy, I tell you I nearly kissed her! Sho' 'nuff, things can change in an instant without any warning," the mom caught Ralph's eyes.

Ralph knew about having your life turned upside down instantaneously. In his entire career at PhasInt, he had never once given thought to leaving. Maybe he had grown too comfortable in his position but he had no reason to think of moving on to something else. Why would he? He understood the culture, contributed to some interesting projects, and knew lots of people in the organization. And, although he only received a 3% increase in his yearly salary increase, he would receive a 10% increase with each promotion. And, the bonuses kept getting better: first, starting with one months' pay when he got into a senior analyst role, to 10% at early management then to 15% with his next promotion, and then 25% of his annual salary at Controller.

By the time he became the General Manager of the European division, he was up to a 40% bonus off of his annual salary. And, when the numbers for the division were good at an EBITDA level, his bonus could be up to 50% of his total salary. Indeed, his expat assignment had been good for his career what with the increase in bonus, tax equalization status, prepaid housing, transportation and schooling allowance for his family and other perks that no US based employee would be privy to.

He was personally looking forward to the day when he would be invited to participate in the company's long term incentive plan that would award him a certain set of stocks based upon company performance and owner approval. Upon formal and successful completion of his expat assignment, he would have been invited into this exclusive club of executives—reserved for really only the top dozen or so. But, since his assignment was cut short and the owner, Vaughn, met him upon his return, he was not extended an invitation. As a matter of fact, neither his salary nor his bonus were increased upon his return to the US and the conditions upon which the bonus rested were a departure from previous years requirements: double digit growth in profit after tax and steady hold on SG&A expenses. Both seemed excessive in the given state of the company's economic status. To Ralph, he still wasn't sure what had gone wrong.

To be clear, Ralph had few regrets about the decisions he had made along the way. He had taken advantage of taking on new assignments and challenging himself to learn, engage, and develop. He wasn't going to leave that to Human Resources to develop himself and his conversation with Laura surely proved that HR was not the answer for employee development. His previous bosses had always admired this trait in Ralph and had told him over and over that there is always a risk in branching out because it doesn't specialize or segment you as a subject matter expert. Ralph felt quite the opposite in that it made him a more complete professional.

Ralph's thoughts lingered on how he got to realize dreams unspoken and unimagined by taking on assignments outside of his comfort zone. In constantly meeting new people, learning new skills, entering new territories, and taking on new assignments, Ralph was able to learn more about venture capitalists and private equity than had he stayed a simple analyst, content with whatever life threw at him.

Looking back, Ralph now doubted briefly if he should have focused on simply one area of expertise and anchored himself to one job or one mentor. Truth be told, so many of the executives who were at PhasInt when Ralph started were no longer there. So, in hindsight, Ralph still believed he made the right decisions for himself and his family.

Or did he? He was not sure he really had a family to go back to anymore. In his desire for achievement, he may have lost everything.

***

DING DING DING!

Ramona let out a raucous laugh followed by a girlie giggle. "Mommy! I did it! I got to level ten!! Come look!" The computer kept dinging to indicate that Ramona had indeed reached a milestone marker for the game. She didn't wait for her mom to look over at the computer screen before fully immersing herself in the new challenges that awaited her in level eleven.

"You're doing it, all right, baby!" Rashida focused back on Ralph. "I know this sounds crazy but I just know that something good is going to come from this," her eyes seemed to pierce into Ralph's soul. She stared so intently at him, searching for affirmation, belief, understanding, empathy.

Ralph was surprised she would be so optimistic. "You've got quite a positive attitude about this."

Relationships and Family Matter

"I have to. If not for my sake, then for the sake of my children. James has been a rock to us. I've not seen him flinch in the face of adversity and he has kept on keeping on, if you know what I mean. He gives me the strength and the courage to carry on and this has helped us grow together as a couple. As a family. We may have lost everything inside our home but we still have each other. And, for the first time since I had my kids, I can actually stay at home for a few weeks and take care of them. Of course, I worry about the money but James' work has been real good about giving him extra shifts. They even took up a collection at work for him and have a little coin jar at the front desk in the building. The building has raised over five hundred dollars for us so far! Can you imagine? I am just overwhelmed at the goodness and generosity of others. People are really helping us by paying it forward." A tear fell from the mom's eyes bypassing her cheek and splashing solidly onto her t-shirt.

"I'm Rashida, by the way." She held out her hand

Ralph grasped it lightly and released it. "I'm Ralph."

Rashida walked over to one of the bookcases lining the wall opposite the computers. "Since I've been here and Ramona has been playing games on the computer, I've been taking some of the lessons the House here makes you take such as computer lessons and financial stability lessons. They really try to make sure that you don't get into a situation like this again. I mean, with deadbeat landlords taking advantage of you and stuff. Thanks to the House, they helped us open our first bank account. Of course, it's got nothing in it yet but I hope to change that when I go back to work."

Rashida picked up a book, held it up to Ralph's face and continued,

"And, I've been looking at some of the books on the shelf. This one has been really helpful to me."

He read the front cover, "*Death and Dying* by Elizabeth Kubler Ross?"

Ralph had noticed the bookcase while he was on the phone but hadn't stopped to look at the unrelated assortment of books on the shelf. He read without verbalizing some of the covers of the books on the shelves: Basic COBOL, Getting Out of Debt, Chicken Soup for the Soul, Housebreaking Puppies, The Complete Guide to Sewing, Your First House, a Bible, The Grace Awakening, Financial Freedom, Why I Believe in Life Beyond Death, and a few dozen more sat waiting to be picked up and read. Most looked like they were used based on the dog-eared covers and scribbles in ink on the binders. Ralph believed they must be donations from people wanting to help contribute to the resources in the House. It was a bizarre compilation of reading material and, turning his attention back toward the book in Rashida's hand, he wondered how Death and Dying had been helpful since no one died in her family fire? Well, other than the dog?

"It talks about the stages of loss and how we are in denial when something catastrophic happens," Rashida's voice got very low and she turned her back on Ramona to ensure the little girl couldn't hear her grown up conversation. "I never would have believed this would have happened to us but it's when life throws you these curveballs, you need to figure out how to hit them and just keep rounding the bases. Reading this book made me realize the different stages of loss and grief and how I can't just deny that I have lost everything I have ever owned. The only thing that was salvaged was Ramona's bicycle and that's only because she left it outside that night. In our neighborhood, you leave anything out at night and it's gone by morning. Heck, it's gone in ten minutes!" Rashida cackled, exposing her wide grin.

"Anyway, what I learned from that book and from my three weeks here in this House is that I have an identity other than my things and that relationships are important. My family is important. I'm spending more time with the girls and James and I are getting along so well. We were talking about splitting up before this happened and now we couldn't imagine going through this alone. I don't know if I am at the point yet to say that this has been a blessing but I honestly never felt that people cared about me before." Tears welled up in Rashida's eyes but did not yet spill over onto her cheeks.

Ralph looked around for a box of tissues but there were none to be had in the mostly barren room.

"I lost my mom when I was just a teenager. I never knew my dad. My grandmother took me in but she was an old lady. I mean, I can appreciate now what she tried to do for me but I was just not interested in going to church, meeting curfew, and following her rules so I left. I got mixed up with a long list of guys who just wanted to use me. I had part time jobs here and there after my first baby was born but the men always took my paycheck to the check cashing place and then exchanged it for weed.'

Ralph fidgeted nervously in his chair.

"I met James through a girl at work. She and I were at the daycare together and he is her brother. He came to pick her up one day and I thought he was like all the other guys but you know what? He wasn't. He isn't. James has been real good to us. He's been with me since Ramona was still a baby and while we used to fight a lot, he treats them like his own. He's a solid man," her voice broke off again and the tears that had formed previously came tumbling down her cheek and dripped off either side of her very angular jaw, her skin stretched taut over either side of her face.

Bony, hollow, and harsh seemed to be appropriate words to describe her, Ralph contemplated. She was definitely in contrast to the delicate, feminine features beholden by Laura.

Ralph detected that her mocha skin was freckled and uneven, containing several small yet elevated moles and bumps as if she was still undergoing a bout of acne from adolescence. Certainly older than a teenager for having at least a five or six year old and one child even older than that, Ralph's mental math would have placed her in her early twenties although her face told a different story.

While Rashida brought her hands to her face to wipe away the saline liquid cascading down, Ralph looked more closely at her overall appearance. Gold nose piercing in her left nostril and massive gold hoop earrings decorated her face. Her straightened black hair was slicked back into a short ponytail that was tightly held together by a green rubber band. Her nails sparkled gold flecks with accents of blue whenever her hand motions caught the attention of the overhead lights. One nail was chipped and in need of repair or being trimmed.

"I'll get you a tissue from the bathroom," Ralph said. It was an opportunity for him to make a break in the conversation that was making him ever so uncomfortable. He hated to see women cry and he really didn't know what to say when she admitted to smoking pot. It was getting pretty hard for him not to form a stereotypical assessment about her.

"Oh, don't worry about it. I think I have a napkin in my pocket from dinner. I've been doing this for the last three weeks. It helps to talk about it, you know? Maybe it's so fresh for you, things haven't settled enough for you. Then again, you're a guy," Rashida didn't give him time to answer. She was taking advantage of having another adult to confide in.

"Mommy! I'm at level eleven! My puppy is getting fat with all the treats she's eating!" Ramona could not contain her zeal. Ralph enjoyed hearing her exuberance. He missed the sound of children laughing.

"Great job, babycakes. Just five more minutes though, you hear? We gotta get you ready for bed," Rashida promised.

"Awww…" Ramona didn't want to rip her eyes from the screen for fear she would miss a tasty treat for her plentiful puppies dominating the computer panel.

Rashida turned back to Ralph. "I don't know about you but me and James are gonna start afresh. Do something new. Live in a different neighborhood. Spend more time with the kids. Maybe even go back to school and be a better provider for my family. If I can say anything it's this: family matters. I never really had one so seeing us come together and having only us—no Xbox or Blu-ray or iPad or all the toys in the world—has meant the world to us. The House is teaching us that."

She looked upward, wistful, with a slight smile on her lips.

"Here, I have to do the homework with the girls, make sure they are dressed and off to the bus on time and take some of the courses to better prepare us for what's next. As a result, I have been having some real good conversations with James about our future. You know, more than what couples normally talk about during the course of day. We never really talked about anything other than right now and living day by day," Rashida finally paused to take a breath before continuing on.

"I see that all of this happened for a reason. I had been ignoring what was really important to me, to us, and what I wanted to do in this life. I think that it took everything being destroyed and getting to the lowest point ever that is forcing us to make a change and that's a good thing. If you don't get to that point, you kind of settle for mediocrity because it's not that bad. Now, we have the opportunity to get out of our neighborhood and really think about what is next for us. You know, have a plan and work towards it. We don't want to live in poverty for the rest of our lives. I certainly don't want that for my girls. Before this, I was always so stressed out and feeling like I never could come up for air. Whatever air I did have, I spent yelling at the girls and James."

Ralph knew that feeling of being yelled at by his wife, the constant bickering and feeling so stressed out that he would suffocate unless he left. Obviously, worlds of economies apart but it seems that the problems don't go away with more money.

"Even though I miss my stuff, the Red Cross has taken care of us real good. I may not be certain about what our future holds but I do know this. This event has changed my perspective on so many things which has helped me to see things differently—for the better. My kids' lives mean something and we are more than just our stuff," Rashida clutched Death and Dying to her chest and looked down at the plastic yellow watch she was wearing. "Oh my goodness, Ramona, close that game down. We need to get you in the bathtub," and then she turned to Ralph. "It was nice talking to you. Good luck on your time here."

Your Identity Is More Than Just "Stuff"

Ramona uttered an "Awww, mom. I'm winning! Do I have to?"

"Yes, you do. Shut it down now. Save the game and you can pick it up where you left off tomorrow. Come on. NOW. Shut it down."

She turned to Ralph "Are you leaving too? We can walk upstairs together," Rashida offered as she ensured that Ramona was logging off of the computer.

"Yup," responded Ralph as they both got up to leave. He had other things he needed to do, too. In fact, her mention of a bath to Ramona made him think that a shower right now sounded pretty good. He imagined he could smell his own BO unless it was just remnants of odor wafting downward from the cafeteria into the computer room. Dinner had stopped being served half an hour ago so Ralph surmised the smell must be coming from him. All the more reason to leave this room and head upstairs.

Chapter Eight

The Cafeteria

Ramona hopped off her chair and took her mom's hand. Both started to walk toward the door but Ralph beat them to it, remembering how difficult it had been for Ramona to open it up on her own.

Ralph didn't know where the stairs were yet; he had taken the elevator every time he needed to move throughout the House even though the building was only three stories tall. He could use the extra exercise.

All three departed the computer room, took a left into the hallway which was almost completely dark given the setting sun, and Rashida pushed open a door under a brightly lit red light marked "EXIT". Ramona let go of her mother's hand and raced up the stairs, pounding her little purple shoes on each stair, jumping with a sense of triumph on the platform that divided the stairwell into two directions.

"Ramona, wait for me when you get to the second floor," Rashida knew her words were falling on deaf ears. She and Ralph plodded up the stairs, without the oomph and energy of a child. The stairwell smelled like newly coated paint and rubber. He surmised it had recently been updated with paint and lights based on the lack of marks along the walls and the brightly shining iridescent lights hoisted onto access tracks spanning the length of each stair unit.

As they approached the first floor, Ralph inquired, "By the way, do you think the cafeteria is still open? I would like to get something to drink before I head up." He also did not want to encounter any awkwardness that might ensue from having rooms right next to each other.

"I don't see why not. The cafeteria is right here on your left," as she pointed to a set of double doors to the left of the stairwell exit. "They are open all night; you just won't be able to get a meal right now. They closed dinner at 6:30 although Mel always tries to keep something left over in case someone gets hungry in the night. I remember when we came in here at 1am, they made us a plate of food but I don't have any recollection of eating or what they gave us. The girls had fallen asleep in the van on the ride over here. Neither of us was hungry but I appreciated the hospitality. I'm sure Mel or whoever is working tonight would get you whatever you need."

She touched his arm lightly as he fully opened the door to exit the stairwell. "Thank you for listening to me. It really helps to talk it over with someone other than James. I'm sure he's getting tired of my crying but I can't have my babies see me doing this. They mean the world to me. And, I just know something good will come from this. I have to believe that."

He couldn't agree with her necessarily so he simply stated, "Have a good night."

Rashida yelled back up towards the stairs, "Ramona Raquel! I told you to wait for me!" Her voice trailed off as the fire exit door closed shut with an audible click.

***

Ralph entered the right side of the double doors of the cafeteria, heard the smooth jazz sounds of Kenny G (for all he knew, it could have been The Yellowjackets) and looked around. The room was larger than he anticipated but then again, if the cafeteria needed to accommodate all of the guests in the House, it needed to be good sized. He couldn't remember if Steve or LaShaun or Laura had mentioned how many rooms the House had or how many people it accommodated but just judging by the number of round tables and chairs seated in the dining room, it was clearly over forty.

The linoleum floors were a playful checkerboard of green and white tiles that seemed to play off of the checkerboard theme of the tablecloths on the round tables with the only difference being their colors of red and white. He deemed it gave the place a whimsical feel of a nostalgic pizzeria joint. Six tables that could hold six or eight chairs fit snugly into the dining area with barely enough room for people to walk by when fully occupied. Two white microwaves sat beneath a massive community board that publicized typical nutritional information about proteins, carbohydrates, and fats.

The kitchen area looked exactly like the one he remembered from his elementary school days, albeit a miniature version. As soon as he walked in, to the left were the caramel-colored plastic trays with the funky edges for easier steering along the metal countertops. The glass panes where he assumed the food was usually heated and ladled but now were empty given that it was way past dinner hours. He noted there was no cash register at the end of the line, as in school, and no little freezer by said cash register where he could reach in to grab a trusty creamy, childhood friend: Nutty Buddy.

Ralph wondered if lunch lady, Mel, as Laura and Rashida referred to her, looked anything like the sassy ladies he recalled from years past who urged him to try the 'turkey hash' or 'add a bowl of soup to your tray'. Or was Mel like the lunch lady portrayed by Adam Sandler in his infamous "Lunch Lady" song fully replete with hair net, sensible shoes, thick stockings to alleviate pressure from varicose veins, and facial mole with a single hair protruding proudly. Ralph had a verbal chuckle at the idea of Adam Sandler's lunch lady eating Navy Bean and then running off at the end of the song to marry Sloppy Joe and live happily ever after. Seemed that being a lunch lady wasn't too bad of a gig.

He craned his neck to see past the counter into the grill area but couldn't see anyone throughout the kitchen area or the dining hall. He noted that the stainless steel shelves, stovetop, and grill glistened in their cleanliness and every countertop, whether a chopping board or food prep area was bereft of even a morsel or crumb. Someone obviously took the time to thoroughly clean this kitchen.

While his eyes did a search of the kitchen, he focused on the inordinate number and variety of spices that lined the back wall of what looked like the vegetable preparation area. Oregano. Dill weed. Mustard seed. Celery Salt. Cumin. Chili powder. Minced onion. Basil. Black pepper. Clove. Vanilla bean. Thyme. Paprika. Cinnamon. It was unusual for his school cafeteria to offer any seasonings or flavorings other than salt or pepper. Then again, this was not a school cafeteria feeding hundreds of cacophonous children and likely not featuring Elio's pizza rectangles and tater tots.

Ralph's mind turned to the precocious child he'd just met, Ramona, whose squeals of delight during her video game time would be exactly one such child taking advantage of the dining services here. More likely, most of the diners were like her mother, Rashida, who were still struggling with loss and anticipating a brighter future. It was ironic to Ralph that the same sweet spice on the spice rack that would make certain foods more palatable was the same name for the beloved pet lost in that family's recent tragedy.

Ralph looked down at the red folder still clutched in his hands and pulled out the sheet of paper on which he'd begun to take down notes. He reread what he'd already written:

- PURSUE YOUR PASSION
- ENGAGE A TRUSTED BUSINESS ADVISOR, COACH, OR RESPECTED ALLY
- STAY AWAY FROM NEGATIVITY
- BE OPEN TO NEW DIRECTIONS

While Rashida was not a professional in the capacity that he, Steve or

Laura might be or have been, he realized that, even in the face of adversity, she, too, was subconsciously following the tenets above as described by the people he'd met earlier in the day.

One, Rashida's passion was her family—something that she really had only now begun to appreciate after almost losing them to fire. Ralph mulled over the irony of having to nearly lose something or someone in order to fully appreciate its true worth and meaning in one's life, just as Rashida did.

Two, she was taking advantage of the resources available to her in the House and for once, opening up to others emotionally not just to survive and tread the waves that seemed to overpower her on a daily basis but actually try to overcome them with the help of trusted allies in the form of the Red Cross, her case worker, and even Ralph.

Three, while certainly sad over the loss of so many material possessions like electronics, clothes, and furniture, Rashida really was not despondent or negative about the situation. In fact, she emphasized time and again how something GOOD was going to come from it. She effused that sentiment with all of her being.

Finally, Rashida's last comments to Ralph were filled with hope about how she and her partner had planned to make a fresh start by moving to a new neighborhood where she would take on a new job, possibly learning some of the life skills taught to her during her three weeks in this House. Of course, she had mentioned that her interest in actively parenting her children may now take a more prominent role in her daily activities.

Not only was Rashida embodying these unspoken rules of loss, she added her own perspective to her situation. And, while she had to voluntarily give up her job in order to deal with the chaos all around her, her loss of job and subsequently income was no less damaging than Ralph's. Given her impoverished financial circumstances, her real life situation was likely more urgent.

Ralph set the folder down on the table closest to the door, pulled a red plastic chair out from underneath the table and sat down. He took out the pen in the folder and added to his list.

- RELATIONSHIPS / FAMILY MATTER
- YOUR IDENTITY IS MORE THAN JUST 'STUFF'

The last line made Ralph wonder how well he and Connie had done with material possessions. Both having grown up in solid middle class families, they knew the value of hard work and a dollar. They tried not to live above their means and keeping up with the Joneses was not especially important to either one of them. They lived in a modest three-bedroom house in the suburbs of Philadelphia which they had moved into after the adoption of Michael. They needed the extra bedroom as an upgrade from their starter town home that was in Conshohocken, only a few exits away. They both liked the feel of being close to neighbors yet having somewhat easy access to Center City for Ralph's work and Connie's occasional desire to partake of the abundant cultural activities throughout the city. That is, if one could call driving on the Schuylkill Expressway 'easy access'.

The house they bought was a stretch for them at the time but Ralph had his sights on being promoted to Controller within the coming years which could justify his six hundred and eighty five thousand dollar mortgage. The bump in salary and bonus would put less of a strain on them once that happened and it was not out of the league for others above him in his department. Several of the VPs at PhasInt lived in homes both on the Main Line and a few miles out that way were upwards of eight and nine hundred thousand.

He had not envisioned an opportunity to move abroad and had that been on his professional dashboard, they might not have been so hasty to buy at the height of the real estate market. As hindsight is 20/20, there was no use in bemoaning an eighteen percent devaluation on the value of their house that would make it ridiculous for them to sell their place come time to move abroad. They didn't want to take such a loss on it and the company certainly didn't offer up a relocation package that included purchasing their home, as he'd heard about from other expats. Furthermore, Ralph and Connie had lazily dreamed about when he would be invited to partake of the company stock plan that then they might consider a move to the Main Line. But, to buy a house for seven figures plus was not only an impracticality, it was an impossibility.

The house was neatly kept by a weekly landscaper who Connie had hired on the recommendations of other neighbors. Ralph wasn't home enough during the weekdays or weekends to mow, prune, or weed the massive 1.3 acre lot and his allergies usually got the best of him regardless of the season. Ragweed, pollen and tree molds sent him into a sneezing frenzy and it wasn't worth his energy to save the $120 / week to have someone else suffer through the misery. Besides, neither Ralph nor Connie possessed a green thumb although she did enjoy buying dozens of trays of annuals each season in order to give the exterior of the house a refreshed look. As fall was soon approaching, Connie would likely make her usual foray to one of the many mom-and-pop nurseries in Montgomery County to purchase a colorful and bountiful array of pansies, violets, mums, and snapdragons. They would soon be replaced once the first snowfall fell and she brought out the decorations for Christmas.

Ralph smiled at the memory of Connie last year trying to carry the forty-pound bag of red mulch from the trunk of her Volvo sedan to the garden areas dotting the lawn. She had driven to the nursery in the morning, spent practically all morning there returning with several varieties of flowers to plant in addition to the cornstalks, pumpkins and hay squares she used to decorate the front porch. She looked au-natural with her graying brown hair peeking outside of her red kerchief tied behind her head, an old flannel shirt awkwardly tucked into tattered khakis that were used only for gardening. She found Ralph watching her from the bay window and motioned for him to come outside and lend a hand with the heavy bag.

She walked to the edge of the yard and with a thick canvas glove on her left hand and tiny garden rake in her right, Connie diligently dug at the soil unearthing her summer series of begonias and marigolds along with impatiens and petunias that had started to develop root rot thanks to the inordinate amount of rain received earlier in the season. They may not live on the Main Line officially, but Connie was resolute in giving the exterior of her home an air of grandeur—at least through the landscaping. Ralph wasn't sure they would be able to afford either the weekly landscaping services or the quarter-annual lawn makeovers now that he was unemployed.

Ralph reflected long and hard about their purchases and personal finances. He had dutifully set aside the requisite 6% of his salary each month on a pre-tax basis for his 401K which was matched by a company contribution of 3% but not to exceed $6000 per year. It only amounted to roughly thirteen to seventeen thousand dollars per year as per maximum federal regulations; he had been faithful to contribute as soon as was promoted into his first management position at PhasInt twelve years ago. The early contributions were measly at his forty-five thousand dollar a year job back then, but with each successive increase, he occasionally was able to stash away larger chunks through additions to an after-tax college fund for Michael.

The last time he received a copy of his 401K statement, his contributions were up to over two hundred and eighty thousand dollars which wasn't bad given his conservative allocation of funds and the dip in the market two years ago. That was in addition to the $20K he had invested in gold at the advice of his father in law last year, another $32K in a private mutual fund based on a small cap international index after he saw the importance of global markets during his twenty four months abroad, and a private money market account he opened as an emergency fund after a tree had crashed onto their garage during one of the mean Nor'easters that had come barreling through the area the first year they had moved into their house. He still had twenty-five years left on his mortgage, which at an interest rate of 6.25% or nearly $4200/month was not in his best interest.

When he was tapped for his overseas assignment, Ralph knew they would ultimately be coming back to the area so they opted not to sell their house. The market was down and the company helped them arrange to rent it out and thankfully paid for the broken lease for the tenants when they called the Pibbs' back to the US. There had been a few decorating items needing to be done and that money market account helped them out time and time again from purchasing new furniture to updating the landscaping that had been severely neglected while they were away, to the out of pocket expenses that needed to be paid for when Michael broke his leg trying to steal second base last year. Ultimately, the account dipped beneath its minimum $10,000 threshold which the bank requested Ralph convert into a regular savings account.

Ralph knew he could routinely put some away into the fund every now and then and so wasn't too worried about it. They weren't swimming in cash, but they weren't hurting either. As long as he had a steady income coming in. Which, now, he did not.

He was glad, at least, that he and Connie had just sent off a check from the money market account to pay for this new year of Michael's schooling at $18,000/year. While Michael had only begun to start kindergarten when they lived in Europe and would have most certainly stayed in the public school system had they not chosen to go abroad, Ralph and Connie decided that placing him in a private school would ease the transition back into the American educational system. He would appreciate the discipline, variety of topics, earlier study of foreign languages, and rigors of a classical, private education. Already, within the year, Michael had shown great promise for assimilating with his classmates and absorbing the curricula. Ralph and Connie were quite pleased with their selection of school and had promised Michael to keep him in the sequestered environment for as long as his grades kept up with the grueling pace—even in the second grade.

The school was always asking the parents to dig in for fundraisers. Ralph never took the time to attend them whether it was a parent/child dance or silent auction or parent mixer although Connie always begged him to attend. "Send them a check, that's what they want anyway," Ralph would respond. Connie, knowing too well that was likely true, would scribble out a four figure sum quarterly to ensure their son would be favorably recognized by the school administration.

There was no way that Ralph could cough up that sort of change in this upcoming school year. The pumpkin patch extravaganza was the first event followed by the annual holiday party after which followed the parent/child Valentine social (where Connie required a new outfit to dance with father and son in their rented tuxes. Ralph admitted, they did look dashing last year!), finally culminating in the end of year silent auction fundraiser.

Further, fall and spring breaks were now starting to be spent at a time-share they had visited once before going abroad that was mommy and child friendly alternating between San Diego and Orlando. Their last time in Orlando—this past April—took them to Universal as opposed to Disney World. Michael declared he was done with the baby rides and wanted something more exciting, like the Harry Potter ride or the Minion Mayhem. The lines were atrociously long but Michael excitedly chattered through the two-hour wait with other excited adolescents as the line meandered through the castle upon which several props from the movie were mounted. Thinking back on the vacation from a financial perspective, the cost of the parks, meals, rental car, flights, parking, and assorted souvenirs set Ralph back an easy $6000 per trip.

This was in addition to the house they rented down the shore in Ocean City, New Jersey. He had only gone down one day this summer with Connie and Michael while they vacationed at the house at the south end of Asbury Street. He couldn't tear himself away from work longer than to spend a Saturday with them and he and Connie were nowhere near close to resolving their differences over his work schedule. Michael had been able to invite two friends with him which lessened the sting of his absent father. Connie invited some friends from church, so it wasn't a total loss. But still, he might not have spent the $4000 on the rental had he known the termination was coming.

Ralph did a mental run through of recent checks Connie relayed to him that they had just written and was thankful that he recalled she'd already sent through the funds to cover October's timeshare in San Diego. After today, he wasn't sure if there would be a spring break activity come next year and not quite sure if he would have the money to afford daily activities in San Diego like surfing lessons, a day at Knott's Berry Farm, a trip to Disneyland and other frivolities like the zoo. It may just be a week spent on the beach with food bought at the local grocery store to make peanut butter and jelly sandwiches with no rental car but a Super Shuttle ride to and from the timeshare. The costs were in the details.

In doing the math, Ralph realized he needed almost eighteen thousand dollars a month in order to keep up with all the family expenses between the mortgage, car payments and insurances, groceries, gasoline, utilities, healthcare, Michael's private schooling, cell phone plans, and vacations not to mention discretionary spending of new clothes for Connie and Michael, presents for birthday parties, weddings, and Bar Mitzvahs of friends and family, and general entertainment expenses like movies, putt-putt, and eating out. Ralph was elated he couldn't add a country club membership to his list of mandatory monthly expenses.

"Whewwwwwww," Ralph let out an audible sigh. If $18,000/month was the net he needed to take home, then adding in the Philadelphia city wage tax of 4.5%, the Pennsylvania state tax of 3% and the Federal income tax rate at 39.6% compounded with the FICA and health insurance premiums added in amounted to a total gross salary needed of at least $350,000/year for basic expenses. He was sure that the COBRA insurance he would be offered in his severance package would significantly increase his out of pocket expenses while he was uninsured.

In looking at the list, Ralph was ashamed of two things. One, that he and Connie had never really sat down to discuss their spending habits and potential areas of financial improvement and opportunity. And two, that they had never drafted a plan in case a steady income wasn't coming in so steadily.

While they didn't really live above their means (they carried a modest credit card balance less than $7,000 between the variety of credit cards, store cards, and loyalty cards), they were really not much different than Rashida and James in terms of living day by day, not proactively plotting out their finances and having a solid back up plan.

Maybe HE needed to take the financial freedom course the House was offering to residents.

Chapter Nine

The Cook

Ralph had tuned out the soft jazz tunes that were prevalent when he first entered the dining area but he certainly heard what sounded like a pot crashing to the floor in the kitchen.

"Hello?" he called out.

A burly man with bulging muscles in his pectorals and biceps appeared in front of the grill but behind the food counter. Ralph would have normally noticed the size of his arms but was further impressed due to his brandishing of a massive metal meat cleaver clenched in his right hand.

"Yeah? What can I get for you?" the man glowered back. He ducked his head underneath the countertop separating Ralph from the kitchen and stealthily appeared, like a ninja, before Ralph within a matter of seconds.

A tight navy blue t-shirt was mostly covered by a white smock that was unbuttoned below where it should have been for good hygiene purposes. The apron was pockmarked with a variety of stains that looked like a bedecked Christmas tree: something red like blood—maybe ketchup; something green like grass, but not; and something brown like dirt, but maybe dried meat or gravy stains, at least as best Ralph could guess. He was a little shorter and lighter than Ralph's height and weight, although the man was certainly in better shape than Ralph. Ralph couldn't even detect a slight tummy paunch through the smock; the veins pulsating from his neck and forearms gave Ralph the impression that this guy is either tenderizing a lot of meat with the free-weight cleaver or performing Rocky Balboa-like boxing feats in the freezer on a slab of beef. Although, looking at him, Ralph felt he'd be better suited for kung-fu kicks on the cow.

Intimated by the sheer force of masculinity in front of him, Ralph stood up to even the playing field with the knife-wielding man standing over him.

Upon arising, Ralph perceived the man's brown eyes slanted into little slits giving him the once over. For sure, Ralph swore he heard the soundtrack to "The Good, The Bad, and The Ugly" somewhere in the background until he realized that it was Cleaver Man whistling a Herbie Hancock tune that was currently coming through the radio waves.

"What can I get for you?" Cleaver Man reiterated. His gray, pencil thin mustache wobbled as his lips pursed his words. He had a light growth of gray stubble covering a few areas of his mostly clean-shaven face. His eyebrows were likewise gray but not as manicured. Ralph imagined it must be difficult for him to get close to another person without poking their eye out with a few errant brows that had to each be two inches long.

"I just came in for something to drink," stammered Ralph.

The man pointed his cleaver toward a glass-enclosed refrigerator just past the massive spice rack. "We've got all kinds of juice, pop, and milk in that fridge over there. What's your preference?"

"I can get it," as Ralph decided to put some distance between him and the massive weapon of individual destruction.

He took a few steps toward the counter before the man blocked further access to the kitchen and said, "No, I can't let you behind the counter. Sanitation regulations. What can I get for you? Would you like a pop?"

Ralph worried how the caffeine might keep him up. "No thanks. What kind of juice do you have?"

"Orange, apple, tomato and cranberry."

"I'll take a cranberry."

Cleaver Man casually ducked back under the counter, approached, and then opened the beverage refrigerator to pluck a can of Minute Maid CranApple juice from the rack. He lowered himself back underneath the countertop to deliver the can, unopened, to Ralph. The cleaver remained glued in his hands at all times. Ralph was impressed with his agility.

"Thanks," said Ralph as he popped the top and took a sip of the sweet and tangy liquid.

"No problem. Can I get you anything else?"

"No, I'm good."

"Okay. The name is Mel if you need anything."

Mel? Lunch lady Mel?

Ralph didn't fathom Mel could be a guy. Then again, neither Laura nor Rashida had mentioned that Mel was a lady, Ralph just assumed so. He certainly bore no resemblance to any of the lunch ladies he knew or the one who ran off with Sloppy Joe.

"You're Mel?" Ralph's tone sounded incredulous.

"Yeah. Melvin Wong. Judging by your reaction, I can only imagine what you've heard about me!" Mel let out an energetic chortle.

"Oh, nothing really," Ralph spluttered.

"Now, I know that's not true! Let's see. You heard about the crazy Asian guy in the cafeteria? Well, I'm sure you heard I make one mean shrimp fried rice!" Mel's glee could not be contained in knowing that others were talking about him. Now, whether that was actually true or not, Mel's ego was certainly big enough to suppose it.

"Not really. I heard I should eat dinner."

"I don't recall seeing you in the dinner line. I have a few leftovers from tonight's meal. We had stuffed cabbage rolls in a creamy, basil tomato sauce with mashed potatoes, gravy, and freshly shelled English garden peas. It was pretty tasty if I don't say so myself. In fact, I don't recall seeing you at all in my kitchen this week. You must be new."

Ralph was impressed with himself that he rightly guessed the majority of stains on Mel's smock.

"Sounds good but I'm not really hungry. The juice will do."

"All the meals here are good and healthy. Your body is a temple; you need to treat it as such. Anyway, welcome to the House." Mel popped the cleaver into his left hand and thrust his now-empty right hand into Ralph's, pumping it energetically. Ralph grimaced at the force of his shake.

"I see you're in pretty good shape with that handshake. Fancy footwork, too, to be ducking under countertops with sharp cutlery."

Melvin grinned ear to ear at that. "It's been a habit of mine for a long time to take care of myself. I really got into a good workout routine during my first layoff. You know, you need to keep a schedule."

Keep A Routine

Layoff? He couldn't imagine how often a line cook got laid off. There were literally hundreds of jobs for cooks anywhere in the city.

"Keeping a schedule?" Ralph couldn't help himself. It was such a strange comment he almost had to inquire.

"Keeping a schedule. It's why I chop my vegetables at night--so I can have my mornings free for tai chi and walk around the neighborhood with my wife. We've become pretty fanatical about our schedules. It provides for efficient processing."

Ralph stared at him, still not understanding what Mel was driving at with his term of 'efficient processing'. Really, how difficult could it be to plan a menu and prepare food?

"During the earlier layoffs, I would get into a good routine only to have it be interrupted when I started up work again. After the fifth layoff, or maybe it was the third termination, I figured this should become a way of life whether I was working or laid off or whatever." Mel rolled his eyes upward and shrugged his shoulders as if being laid off five times or fired three wasn't a big deal.

"I don't think I follow you," a perplexed Ralph declared. He quietly opined that this guy must be really difficult to work with if he kept getting fired from his jobs, no matter how good or healthy his food was. He took another sip of his juice.

"The IT world is really unstable. You never know if you're coming or going. Whether it's a start up, mid cap, or established multinational, the IT department usually has the most fluctuation in terms of retention and employee satisfaction. We are always the last to know of any issues but the first to be held accountable. And, the first to be expendable, if you know what I mean."

Ralph considered his own experience with IT, which was relegated only to opening a query when his laptop froze up or set up encryption for highly confidential communications. He did note that the person who came to fix his computer each time was a different face but he never equated that with a high turnover or employee satisfaction rate. He was too junior at PhasInt to say he lent a hand in the migration to a new accounting reporting system way back when but recalls what a fiasco that was. The delays, bugs, and errors that were caused culminated in the termination of the key leads of the IT implementation team. But, what did IT have to do with a cook?

"I'm sorry, Mel. I don't understand where you are going with this," Ralph said flatly.

Mel teased, "I may look like a cook to you but I am a covert IT operative. Ha ha ha! Actually, my background is in technology and over the last fifteen years I've been out of work almost as often as I've been at work. You go from being overly busy with an overcrowded calendar that is insanely intense to an environment where no one returns your phone calls or responds to your emails. It's like going from hero to zero overnight. The stress of being out of a job can be so physically and emotionally damaging that I wanted to make sure that I was taking care of myself by eating right, sleeping well, making sure I was getting steady exercise. I had so much more energy which gave me the ability to deal with the negativity that just confronted me when I wasn't getting any responses to job queries, recruiters weren't returning my calls, and even friends seemed to avoid me. I figured out a while ago that if I wasn't being challenged mentally, I needed to do something for myself physically."

Ralph admired Mel's dedication to his body and took a breath in to minimize his own gut.

"The continual uncertainty of IT projects within any given organization doesn't make for a stable environment for any of us. So, you learn over time to become very resilient and humble although those first few times you find yourself without a paycheck, you begin to doubt yourself. You think you are damaged, broken, or unemployable and that you have no value to add to your company. That was my case the first few times I was let go. I had to get over the feeling of worthlessness and realize that I can contribute positively and that I am professionally competent both as an IT leader and a provider for my family."

Mel took a breath and continued, "It was tough a few times when my kids were younger and going to college, especially when I was in middle management IT jobs. I've been at all levels of IT from programmer to interim CIO and executive CTO at my last gig. While I was in between work, I had the freedom to explore the limits of my body both mentally and physically. At the end of my times in transition, I couldn't believe what I could do with an agility ball. I mean, I have always been physically active but during these times of transition, I went all out with yoga, Pilates, kickboxing, and running. Now that I am semi-working again, I've promised my wife that I wouldn't let myself go as I'd done when I went back to office work. Working here on a part time basis has enabled us both to remain physically active and even better yet, to do it together. My old lady looks just as good as me!" Mel roared, puffed his chest and pointed his index finger at himself.

Ralph was curious to know more about Mel's past in IT and why he had been let go so many times but didn't want to be rude. He softly inquired, "Why were you involved in so many terminations and layoffs?"

Mel was glad to share his history and pulled out the chair to Ralph's left to sit in. "Well, looking back, part of it was my fault and part of it not my fault. There really are only five ways in which an employee is terminated or let go. The first is obviously for cause. And, I admit I had a few of those. But, the majority are not for cause—I'm speaking mostly about the executive level. I did some pretty stupid things early in my career but learned some great lessons from that which helped fuel my development and maturity. In my experience, executives are pretty self-disciplined people and don't need anyone to hold their hands. So, when they are let go, it usually isn't for performance."

"So, what are the rest?" Ralph asked.

"There's the easy ones like a new leadership team has come in above you and they want to clean house or engineer an internal re-organization caused by a number of factors—usually someone else's poor performance that affects you—that can also relate to new leadership. Mergers and acquisitions are big reasons for layoffs, and while you might think that's relegated to small to medium companies, every company claims victims because of this. A key one, however, is personality conflict. Something might have been going well for a while but then something happens; you do something or not, your boss has unspoken plans or motives and what used to be a good working relationship sours," Mel waxed on.

"You missed one," Ralph urged.

"Right. That's the scapegoat. You did nothing wrong. You were just in the wrong place at the wrong time." Mel nodded his head in agreement to no one other than himself before continuing.

"Yup, I've experienced all of them in my day. The most difficult ones are the ones where the relationship turns and you don't really know why. I had one boss tell me I was being let go for performance issues yet I never had a bad performance review ever. I learned later on from a recruiter that it was a personality conflict and I just never knew. You might never know why. But, you can't beat yourself up with the woulda, coulda, shoulda beens. You just gotta move on and recognize these warning signs of potential disruption to you. That's why I am fanatical about keeping my schedule in working out, staying busy, and even in finding additional employment."

Ralph considered his own experience. It seemed to match that of Mel's wisdom in that there had been new leadership at the top coming in. But, Ralph was under the impression that his owners wanted him to be the right hand to many of the new executives coming in. You know, show them the ropes.

Ralph voiced his opinion to Mel. "Yeah, but what about if all that happens and leadership wants you to lead them through the change?"

Mel wryly smiled, his tiny mustache stretched across his face, "Well, that depends on how involved you'll actually be and the relationships you'll develop. If you have a supportive boss who includes you in the go-forward strategy and you are given challenging responsibilities and the authority in which to accomplish those tasks, I think you'll have no problem. But, if the relationship is strained for whatever reason and you are omitted from key events, let's just say the writing may be on the wall."

Ralph pursed his lips. He wasn't given much time to develop a relationship with his new boss before being let go. But, he distinctly recalled walking by the boardroom or the executive conference room several times in the last month only to see his boss with other key members of his peer group engaged in intense conversation. When Ralph inquired what the meetings were about and if he should be included, he was always met with, "The topic didn't concern your area of responsibility" or "This is a special project that only involves the General Managers". Wasn't Ralph a General Manager? If so, why was he being excluded?

"So, is there anything that can be done to reverse the 'writing on the wall'?" Ralph wanted to know what he could have done differently in his own situation.

Mel furrowed his brow and smacked his lips together before responding. "If you haven't already got solid allies pitching for you or you've uncovered a new way to generate incremental and immediate revenues for the company then generally not. Once a decision has been made about an employee at the highest levels, it is only a matter of time. The next thing the employee needs to think about is on what terms do they want to leave and ensure they've already been actively engaging their network. Sometimes leaving with an air of grace as opposed to making a statement is the better choice."

"What did you do?"

Mel guffawed and grinned a smile so big, it made his eyes invisible. "Ha! Oh, I've done them all. When you're young and brash, your bravado gets in the way. I've called my former bosses nasty names to their faces on my way out the door. I've sent emails to my employees complaining of my terrible treatment. I wrote anonymous and scathing online reviews of the company, even exposing vulnerabilities for 'clients to be aware'. But, I learned that I was only hurting myself. Once I reached forty and then eclipsed fifty, a certain humility and dignity comes over and I just needed to swallow my pride to see to the legal conversation. How much severance was I going to get? What types of benefits accompanied? Would I get paid in one lump sum or a monthly allotment until I found my next position? Were my legal fees paid? Would they offer an outplacement firm? These are all pretty standard questions one should be asking while they are kicking you to the curb."

Swallow Your Pride

"Boy, you got that right," Ralph agreed.

"Got what right?" It was Mel's turn to inquire.

"Kicking you to the curb," Ralph mumbled.

"At some point, you get used to it. I mean, you can't take it personally. From another viewpoint, it keeps you humble but you need to be grounded enough to know that this is not necessarily a reflection on who you are. I know I contributed great things to all these companies. At some, I pointed out errors that the board didn't want exposed as they would have been expensive to fix, both financially and reputationally. In fact, one of the owners of a company I worked for as CIO hadn't read a report that was going to be critical to his operation once I joined the firm. I ended up piecing everything together and pointing out his omission only to realize that it probably wasn't going to end well for me. I remember the day I sat in my office thinking, what should I do? Do I do the right thing? Do I make the best decision for my career and income? I knew I had to do the right thing for both the company and the clients by fixing the product regardless of the cost and was let go for doing what was right -- right now and in the long run. In retrospect, I'm glad I was fired as I'm not sure how long I would have stayed and left on my own.

Situations like that can get depressing but you need to realize it's not you. Myopia is rampant with the current global economic situation."

"So, how did you end up here? Chopping broccoli isn't I.T."

"No. But I'm one damn good cook! Well, that and jobs at my level are hard to find and I'm not the only one looking. The competition is pretty fierce these days with so much talent in the pool but using my talent for cooking keeps my schedule busy while I am looking for that 'right' opportunity. Remember, it's all about keeping a schedule even if you think it's beneath you. At some point in your career, you will need to humble yourself. In so doing, you can't let yourself get down. It's a delicate balance. That's where keeping to your schedule calibrates you," Mel explained.

"Were you this regimented in your jobs?" Ralph speculated.

"Not as much as in the latter years. I think it's an acquired skill. What I have learned, however, is that those who have a plan and stick with it are invariably more successful than those without a plan. Whether you are in transition or taking on a new role or already established in a role, you gotta have a plan. Here, for example, we are a smaller organization without the same resources people might be accustomed to at a large, for profit organization. I needed to know what are the most important things that need to be done in 30 days? These are not my ideas but your potential new boss'. What are the priorities and problems? Go to the direct report. Interview them. Go to your peers. What worked? What didn't? That's the first 30 days. A lot of people fail in the new job almost right off the bat because they did not have a plan. What is critically important/ What are the top things that need to be done. Ask the right questions and you'll get the right answers."

"You sure have a long history. I would have never guessed that from your smock and cleaver in hand! I guess you can't judge a book by its cover," exclaimed Ralph.

Mel appreciated the comment. "No, you can't. And, let me share that there have been times when I have also voluntarily walked away from organizations knowing they were not the right fit for me. Like the time I was asked to implement a program that would have hidden the true revenues of the company in a particular division by funneling money offshore. Or the time I worked for a healthcare company who just could not spend the money on email encryption and training for staff in order to fully comply with HIPPA regulations. That's a big no-no and I didn't want my name on some of these things. Mostly, though, I waited for the axe to fall after taking jobs that I knew were not right for me but I needed the money. My wife wished my career had been more stable."

"Hence, the need for a schedule? To keep the stability?" The underlying premise was starting to make sense to Ralph.

"I guess so. I never thought about it like that but you need something to hold on to. I do a lot of consulting work now as it fits into my schedule. It actually is helpful because I can pick and choose the projects on which I want to work. When you work for a company, you may have a fantasy that you are 'safe' but one, you never really are and two, you are bound by their regulations and the personalities who make them up. At least now I have the freedom to make intelligent choices that interest me for the work to be done as well as the pay. I made the decision to go into independent consulting for all these reasons and more. I enjoy it as I focus exclusively on information security, proposal management for federal contractors, applying for patents and doing some pro-bono work to make the internet safer for small companies. Granted, I'm not making as much as I used to but I get to spend time with the wife, help out here, and stay in shape. It's all a trade off," Mel inhaled deeply and paused. "Why do you ask all these questions?"

"I just got fired today so this is all fresh for me," Ralph's stomach gurgled loudly.

Mel was unsympathetic. "That's life. You can't dawdle on this. But, first things first. You should have something to eat. Let me go make you a plate. I'll be right back," and with that, Mel did a running duck back underneath the counter that could have nearly decapitated him.

Even though he was not mentally hungry for food, Ralph didn't feel like arguing with Mel and turned his attention back to his juice. The cool fluid was like a downpour that hydrated parched and barren land. He could feel his mouth coming alive with the intense flavors of fruitiness; he hadn't anticipated the rush of saliva that stormed his mouth. In a matter of six refreshing gulps, his drink was done.

Ralph needed a bottle of water to infuse some equilibrium between the sweet and sour ratio currently invading his tongue. He shouted, "Mel, can you bring me a bottle of water too?"

Mel reappeared momentarily with requested bottle of water and a heaping plate of stuffed cabbage rolls in hand. He picked up a plastic knife and fork from the front of the cafeteria line and placed the plate in front of Ralph. "Here, enjoy."

Ralph felt obliged to at least take a bite of the food Mel had prepared. The aroma from the tomato sauce drifted upwards and a spiral of steam erupted from the cabbage when Ralph cut into it. A mixture of beef, onions, garlic and white rice cascaded into the tomato sauce splashing a bit onto the tablecloth.

"How is it?" Mel leaned over him.

"I haven't taken a bite yet," Ralph wasn't sure if Mel was hanging around to finish his stories of transition and termination or to gain approval for his cuisine. He took a quick bite just to appease Mel so he could go back to doing whatever it is that he does 'on schedule'.

He popped a forkful of cabbage, meat and sauce in his mouth. It was savory. "It's good," Ralph remarked while chewing.

"Good. I'm glad you like it. Now, going back to your situation: let me give you this advice. Negotiate for life insurance in your package. I'm older so I know this stuff but most people don't realize that they are part of a group policy and now that you are no longer employed you will need to have it. This topic has a low level of consciousness and it doesn't happen very often but it can be catastrophic for the family. If you are unsure of your offer, have an employment attorney look it over. You look over forty so there are certain considerations for us older guys. You'll automatically be eligible to sign up for COBRA for health insurance but really, heed my words on the life insurance. It happened to one of the guys I know from SIM and it was devastating for his family and they had no backup income source."

Ralph didn't appreciate the age reference but hadn't considered life insurance. "Good point," he murmured. He wondered what else he should expect as part of his severance package, and, by the way, what was SIM?

Before he could ask, Mel finished, "I gotta get back to my chopping but, before I finish my prep for the weekend, I want to share one more item with you. After you have failed at jobs as many times as I have, you look back over your career with objectivity. There is a huge difference between failing at something and being a failure. Most successful people fail but they pick themselves up, dust themselves off, and go on to the next thing. The fact that people fail doesn't destabilize them for very long. The experience of failing at something doesn't make you a failure as a person, a provider, or a professional. Embrace the humility and learn from it. This is a key component that you will need to accept as you move forward." Mel looked hard at Ralph to ensure he was 'getting it'.

Ralph nodded.

"I've had periods where the stress from no income coming in was extremely tough on my family. My son was in college, my daughter in high school and as a parent, you feel ashamed that you can't get them the things you used to. But, they know the situation and they are just as much a part of this. Lean in to them for support, for encouragement and trust. No one will be there for you like your family and you are all in this together. It's a humbling experience for everyone but you grow closer as a result," Mel finished his sentence by softening his facial expression and looking out the window.

"Thanks." The reality of the sentiment of family support landed in his belly. Ralph certainly hadn't been a support to his family over the last few months. He wasn't hungry at all now even though his first few bites had been pleasing on the palate.

"I don't know what happened to you and I don't want to know but the best advice I can give you is to stay focused, have a routine, stay positive. You will go through ups and downs but you must remember that this is not about you. This is not your fault. You may be a victim of circumstance but you are not a victim. You have to take yourself away from the negativity and put your energy toward finding the next thing. That means keeping a schedule. And, I've got to keep mine. I'm sure I'll see you in the lunch line some days."

Mel didn't offer to shake Ralph's hand. He simply walked away leaving Ralph with a plate full of food and a room filled with the essences of stuffed cabbage rolls and smooth jazz.

Chapter Ten

The Radio

Mel disappeared back under the counter, behind the grill and into the room adjacent the kitchen where the freezer and food prep stations were. He shut the door behind him in anticipation of closing down for the evening and the night shift that came on to look after the new guests who would likely arrive in a daze—not fully comprehending the likely disastrous events that would make them partake of the House's offerings—including a hot cooked meal upon arrival.

Ralph looked down at his partially touched plate of food in front of him. He swirled the mashed potatoes with his fork, building a little volcano into which the gravy was intermixed. He licked his fork and put it down before reaching for his red folder with previous notes contained therein.

A loud wail of saxophone came through the radio as the smooth jazz sounds turned to cool jazz with Chick Corea gracing the airwaves in the cafeteria. Apparently, the deejays change shifts starting at seven o'clock on Friday nights in preparation of getting the weekend off on a positive groove. The cafeteria, empty except Ralph, was emitting a funky beat.

Tapping his toes, he pushed his plate aside and opened the folder. He didn't want his notes to look like Mel's smock—stained and grubby. Taking out the sheet of paper on which he'd previously written Ralph reviewed his list again.

- PURSUE YOUR PASSION
- ENGAGE A TRUSTED BUSINESS ADVISOR, COACH, OR RESPECTED ALLY
- STAY AWAY FROM NEGATIVITY
- BE OPEN TO NEW DIRECTIONS

- RELATIONSHIPS / FAMILY MATTER
- YOUR IDENTITY IS MORE THAN JUST 'STUFF'

He picked up the pen stuck inside the folder and added the pearls of wisdom just bequeathed by Mel.

- KEEP A ROUTINE
- SWALLOW YOUR PRIDE

Ralph was mesmerized by the stories of tenacity and termination that Mel told—and all of them were about Mel! Ralph couldn't imagine enduring—how many were there?—seven, eight or more firings or layoffs. He was having difficulty with warping his brain around one.

But, since Mel had brought up the five reasons for termination and the rationale that accompanied them, Ralph believed that he may have serendipitously avoided a termination last year when he was called back to the US. Either that or it may have been the precursor and forewarning that ultimately should have prepared him for the events of earlier today.

***

When Ralph touched down in Philadelphia on that Thursday afternoon last year, his company owners had sent a limo to pick him up at the airport to take him to Vontre—the most difficult restaurant reservation in the city. Being summoned back to HQ with a last minute request for a dinner meeting after an eight-hour flight was an anomaly. Ralph knew it meant either really great news or really terrible news.

Ralph's limo pulled up to the restaurant where one of the owners of PhasInt, Barry, was waiting inside. He greeted Ralph warmly upon entering but did not extend his hand for a shake but rather motioned Ralph to take a seat opposite him.

Barry, who was the most reclusive of the "Trinity", actually had very little interaction with Ralph unless there was a discrepancy in one of the reports or a continuing declining trend in profit after tax. He was a distinguished gentleman: tall, pale, usually dressed in a baggy navy blue suit with a thin, multi-color diagonally striped tie; extremely polite, with a prominent nose that held up Coke-bottle, black rimmed glasses that accentuated the fullness of his face. As he is always traveling on an airplane covering huge swaths of distances, he is prone to sinusitis and therefore always carries a proper handkerchief which is neatly displayed in his front right pocket. Rumor had it that he was raised a young boy of privilege and therefore extremely particular about his foods; the choice of this restaurant was not by accident. In fact, wine lists were to be pre-approved before reservations were set and the admin staff had to scour the city for locales with exotic menus--the more outlandish the better. Goat entrails, anyone?

The menu at Vontre certainly didn't disappoint with their selections of pork jowl, lamb neck and pig trotter on this day's menu. Ralph thought, isn't that food that's normally thrown away? Or at least given to the poor in certain countries? But here, this type of food is celebrated for all the fancy ingredients that accompany.

Ralph ordered the imported bufala ricotta with cracked black pepper and vowed to eat the entire portion. In fact, even before Ralph stepped foot into the hard-to-come-by-reservations restaurant, Ralph committed to order an appetizer, entree, and dessert, but not only that, to enjoy them all. For, an occasion like this was not a run of the mill meal—either in degustation or circumstance.

Barry ordered the mortadella mousse as an appetizer and the house special of the night: a $75 plate of truffles and pappardelle in a heavy chanterelle and cream sauce. The men exchanged pleasantries for a few moments. Barry, not being the type to divulge personal information, talked about his recent trip to a remote site in Africa where his wife accompanied. Ralph had met her only once before during a dinner for the European leadership team, and, like Barry, she seemed rather aloof and unwilling or unable to socially mingle with the teams that supported her husband's organization. Ralph cut short the chatter realizing he wasn't here to talk about spouses, travels, or the upcoming holidays. Although, Ralph really wasn't sure what the discussion content was to be so he shut up and waited for Barry to speak first.

Barry began, "Ralph, you know we placed you in Europe to get that division started. The past three years have been very tenuous in the US markets and our best chance for continued prosperity lies outside America."

Ralph nodded.

"With costs as they are for expatriate assignments and anticipating some upcoming changes in the organization, it is important that we keep you fully focused and an integral part of the team," Barry stated.

Ralph nodded again not sure where the conversation was going. The waiter approached the table with the appetizers. Barry immediately attacked his plate using a variety of paraphernalia from fork to spoon to bread. Ralph scooped up a ball of the bufala cheese in his spoon.

"This is to say that Vaughn, Paul and I have taken a decision to return you to the US where you will be the most helpful in these upcoming changes that will be announced shortly. We want to ensure that you are prepared for the next challenges within the organization and fully utilizing your professional repertoire."

Ralph had already scooped up two more spoons full of cheese when he stopped mid-bite. "If I understand you correctly, sir, you are calling me back to the US? By when do you want me back?"

"Yes, that is correct. We can discuss the exact timings as I know you have some personal considerations with your family but the short answer is, the sooner the better. I would give you thirty days to resume residency back at headquarters in Philadelphia."

Thirty days? To move his family back? To tie up recently started projects? To complete the grooming of his successor which wasn't slated to be finalized until next year? Impossible, thought Ralph.

"I'm not sure if I can accomplish everything within that framework, Barry. I mean, that's really aggressive. I have the opening of the office in Vienna, the audit issue in Madrid, and the wrongful termination lawsuit by a former employee in London. It won't be easy to extricate me from these activities."

Just listening to all the activities instilled a sense of fear yet pride in Ralph. One, could he reasonably accomplish everything that was needing to be done and two, my, how he had diversified his career over his near two decades at PhasInt. Ralph had been told previously by his mentors and champions that continuing to reach out to other departments would bring new assignments and knowledge about the business. This would make him a stronger and more comprehensive professional because of the broad background he would attain. However, in a highly specialized company like PhasInt where new MBAs were popping up everyday—many of them with years of experience in a single category like tax, treasury, or mergers—might make Ralph vulnerable to when subject matter expertise was prized more highly than general management.

Ralph had never before worried about his longevity with his company. He viewed it as a strength. And, his loyalty was undeniable. Even knowing that being offshore during his expat assignment might make him less visible in the short term would make Ralph more prominent in the long term. Everyone knew that expats were specifically chosen for greater purposes later on.

By now, Barry had wiped his plate clean with the last of the spongy focaccia that accompanied his first course and chased it down with a glass of the Drouhin Charmes Chambertin pinot noir specifically recommended by the waiter who had now come to remove their plates. Ralph still had a few bites left on his dish but allowed the waiter to clear the table before bringing out the entrees. The waiter returned to scrape off any bits of bread littering the fine linen.

Barry leaned in towards Ralph, elbows placed on the table. "Ralph, your family can take as much time as they need to return to the US. You, however, will be back in Philadelphia within thirty days. There are projects that will be started that you must oversee and our timeline cannot be changed."

Ralph was not sure if this was good news or not. "Can you tell me a little more about these projects and what I will be doing?"

"At this time, no. But, know that we have invested a lot in you and your development and we need you back in the US. I trust that you will do all that you can to meet this deadline."

The waiter arrived with the $75 plate of pasta. Barry licked his lips and could hardly contain his enthusiasm once the dish was released from the waiter's grasp. He didn't wait for Ralph's food to be set down before commencing to shove forkfuls of mushrooms, sauce, and noodles into his mouth, a brown, buttery, and creamy glob of goo oozing down his chin.

Ralph's food was placed before him but he was not so excited by his selection or future. Clearly, the conversation was now over as Barry closed his eyes to savor the flavor of swine-sought fungi. The only thing Ralph could think about was setting a plan to ensure he met the stated timeline.

Both men eschewed dessert and coffee. The main purpose for the flight, dinner, and conversation was past; there was no need to prolong the episode for either one of them. Barry asked for the check and they both caught cabs to their respective destinations.

"I look forward to seeing you next month, Ralph," Barry said through the window of his taxi right before it pulled away and down Thirteenth Street.

***

Ralph looked down at the mess he'd made of the cabbage, potatoes and meat on his plate and decided to call it a night. He stood up, picked up the plate and walked it to the garbage can where he tossed it in, being careful not to have the gravy or tomato sauce splash on to the surrounding walls. Or himself. He may be smelly from having been in his suit all day but he didn't need to further recklessly ruin it.

He seized the papers spread out before him and neatly tucked them into the red folder. He vaguely noted a Michael Jackson tune in the background judging by the number of "HEEs" and "HOOs" that were audible:

"If you wanna make the world a better place
Take a look at yourself, and then make a change"

Ralph had never been a huge fan of the late MJ although he had spent a few school dances boogying to the likes of "Off The Wall" and "Thriller". While he knew a few of the choruses of the more popular songs, "Beat It" was the only one he knew most of the words to. And, that was really only because Weird Al Yankovic had parodied it so much and actually enunciated the words so that Ralph could make out most of them. MJ's tunes were catchy but lent the listener more toward dancing than singing along. Ralph was sure millions of King of Pop fans would scold him for such a sentiment.

He clutched the folder to his chest in an attempt to get up and walk to his room but his legs weren't moving. He felt a tightness in his throat and chest as he found himself mouthing the chorus to *The Man in the Mirror.*

The words shattered Ralph's previous understanding of this song being about just a homeless man. His dreams had been washed out. His heart had been broken as well as him breaking the heart of the one he held most dear. Had he become like MJ's man in the mirror who had no place to go? Would the next step be one that he would have to initiate in order to get back what he had lost?

Ralph didn't need to contemplate the irony of the lyrics any further and burst through the doors of the cafeteria with the full intent of getting to his room before he could hear another crotch-grabbing HEE. He was in fear of losing control of his emotions and did not want Mel or Rashida or any other guest or worker in the House to see him succumb to tears.

He'd already gotten halfway down the corridor, blindly aiming for his room when he realized he wasn't one hundred percent sure where his room was or how to get back there. Laura had told him how to get there from his room but he had arrived at the cafeteria from downstairs via the stairwell; he had descended to the ground floor via the elevator. It didn't make sense for him to walk all the way back downstairs, across the building to find the elevator to take back up to the second floor. He stopped in his tracks to get his bearings before barreling through the House any further.

At the intersection where the stairwell met the corridor, Ralph took a deep breath, composed himself and looked around. The hallway curved to the left while the stairs descended to the right. Ralph peeked around the corner and saw another hallway lined with paintings, drawings, and sculptures. He hoped he saw the reception area at the end of the way.

He slowly started proceeding down this corridor hoping he was going in the right direction. Maybe this would be the way?

A picture of a red house with a cascade of fluorescent pink and yellow flowers out front and a fluorescent orange sun in the sky was so bright, his eye was naturally drawn to it and he slowed the pace of his walk down considerably, taking time to peruse the art on either side of the hallway. This one looked like it had been colored using highlighter pens.

Other pictures depicted stick-figure families, likely drawn by elementary students while others were brightly colored, ornately drawn mosaics. One caught his eye of a little boy at bat. It reminded him of Michael who had a series of little league games tomorrow, Saturday. Ralph was glad this was not his official weekend to take Michael but had mentioned in casual passing he would 'try' to make it to his games this weekend.

Both Connie and Michael knew 'try' meant 'usually not'. At least Ralph wouldn't be in hot water that he couldn't get out to the suburbs. With no access to his car keys, he couldn't very well travel outside of the city. His house wasn't on a public transportation line and he didn't have the funds on hand to take an expensive taxi ride. He couldn't show up and ask Connie to pay for it—that would invite conversations he wasn't prepared to have right now.

Ralph mentally elaborated on what Mel had said about his own family: that they were the support system for him and rallied around him during his various rounds of professional elimination. After having rejected Connie and Michael so many times over this past year in favor of an organization who clearly held no regard for Ralph, would they take him back? Could they re-strengthen the bond they used to share? It may be easier with Michael than with Connie. Kids were much more malleable, forgiving and open than adults.

Ralph tightly squeezed his lids closed in order to hold back the sting of tears that were imminent to fall from his eyes.

Chapter Eleven

The Director

Ralph heard a door close loudly and looked up to see a large yet impeccably dressed man exiting a door approximately thirty feet away. The man popped his keys in the door, jiggled the handle and waved at Ralph.

Ralph looked behind him to see if the man was waving at someone else.

"Have a good night!" the man called out.

Ralph looked behind him again to see if the man was talking to someone else down the hallway. "Are you speaking to me?"

The man approached Ralph, apparently intent on forcing a conversation. "Yes, I was. I see you admiring the artwork. Many of them are done by the children of the victims of disaster from the city."

Ralph looked up to see the very large, very dark, very bald man smiling down on him. This was no little feat given Ralph's six-foot stature and ample girth, himself. Between Mel's macho muscles and this man's immense stature, Ralph was feeling a bit more insecure.

The man pointed to a picture depicting gold nuggets around what looked to be Fort Knox. "If you look closely, you can see the template indicating the artist and his or her age. We partner with an organization named Fresh Artists to supply the artwork. Fresh Artists is an organization comprised of young people who have been displaced by disaster."

They both stood in silence for a moment.

"I don't think we've met yet. I'm Charles Davis."

"Ralph Pibbs."

"You must be new. I know everyone staying with us. Did you just arrive today?"

"Yes." Ralph didn't feel compelled to give away any more information. He was exhausted and really just wanted to get to his room before someone saw him lose it. He reeked of BO and cabbage thus necessitating a bar of soap to be scoured across his body. It may only be eight at night but he could fall into a deep slumber until his credit cards arrived in the morning.

Furthermore, Ralph didn't know Charles' connection to the House. On the other hand, Charles was obviously attired well enough that he couldn't have been a resident. Or could he? Ralph did not notice a placard on the door indicating it was an office.

"It's amazing to see how these youngsters can still have a positive outlook and create something so beautiful out of something so catastrophic in their lives," Charles mused. "We use art as a therapy to help young people particularly work through their trauma. And, you can see the results are fantastic! Look at the use of color here," as Charles pointed across the hall from his office to a bountifully ornate watercolor depicting a fire hydrant that was spewing forth flowers.

"Do you work here?" Ralph felt Charles knew a bit too much about the artwork, programs, and protocols to merely be a resident.

"I do beg your pardon!" Charles exclaimed apologetically. "Yes, I am the executive director of the Red Cross House. I should have stated that when I started talking to you out of the blue." Charles' hand was extended, waiting for Ralph to take it.

Ralph immersed his hand in Charles', his entire wrist swallowed up by the bigger man's grip. How tall was he? Six six? Taller? The man was ginormous enough to be a defensive tackle for the Philadelphia Eagles.

"I was just leaving for the evening but please, come on inside. I make it a point to welcome everyone personally," Charles reproduced his key and inserted it into the lock on his door.

"Oh, I don't want to bother you. I was just heading up to bed myself," Ralph lightly protested.

Charles didn't seem to hear him and ushered Ralph in by standing behind him as he eased the door open.

"I'm sure you've met your case worker already. How has your experience been so far?" Charles motioned for Ralph to sit in the plush leather chair opposing a massive desk that filled up a good 2/3 of the cramped office.

"Laura was great. Yeah, everyone has been really nice. Mel is quite the character. I didn't know the Red Cross offered something like this," Ralph found himself talking more than he wanted to and he noticed a number of articles and photographs posted around the tiny office walls. There were a few citations from the Mayor and City Council in addition to numerous newspaper and local magazine articles about Charles, the House, and several of the residents.

"Good. I'm glad to hear that. One of the things we try to foster here is a spirit of collaboration where everyone's best skills are brought to the forefront for the sake of our guests. We specifically seek out folks who are passionate about helping others and being part of a positive environment." Charles eased himself into the leather chair behind his desk.

Passion and positive. Ralph thought of Steve and Laura. Well, Charles was two for two on that.

"And, in terms of the support you have received so far? We do run a pretty tight ship here so you'll be subjected to a scheduled routine of meal times, mandatory classes, and locked doors. It's our aim to get people back on a right track; sometimes that means looking at new directions."

"That's an interesting concept. I mean, the classes and the new directions," Ralph was referring to Rashida and how the classes, support, and daily schedule had already seemed to have made an impact in her life.

"Absolutely. We have seen lives transformed by adhering to a series of simple principles. In the ten plus years that we have been serving the people of Philadelphia, thousands have come to us with nothing, yet left with something more valuable than money can buy," Charles' pride was protruding.

"What's that?" Although Ralph had a pretty good idea just based on his conversations with the people he had met thus far.

"Self dignity. Self respect. Self-awareness. All of these attributes about self are what make us who we are, how we act towards others, and the reactions we exude when we encounter difficult circumstances. Just take yourself, for instance."

Ralph wasn't sure where Charles was going with this. He was sure Charles didn't have a file on him to verify the facts of today's events which alone included being fired, burning down his apartment, and becoming homeless.

"You are here obviously under great duress. No one comes to us out of voluntary choice. You are here because some external disaster caused you to be displaced. And, we are here to help you overcome and exceed the challenges set before you," Charles looked at Ralph very intently.

"There will be a few lessons that you will take with you once you move on from the Red Cross House," Charles continued.

Ralph opened up his folder to see if Charles was going to list any of the eight items he'd learned thus far. "Well, I've been making a list. Let's see what you can add." Ralph was drawn in to the conversation although he was so exhausted and wanted to head to bed.

"One is it's never too late or too early to start networking. We are all interconnected and it doesn't matter that you got here by happenstance. It matters what you do with what you learned, who you met, and how you will apply that to your life. You can see from the photos and articles all around this office how critical it is to stay connected to others. Networking—whether professional or personal—is a key to keep you connected."

Network, Network, Network!

"What's the other?"

"Have faith—good will come from this," Charles leaned back in his chair. "There is nothing more powerful to the human spirit than hope. You have to believe that good indeed will come from this."

Ralph felt the lump return to his throat. He pulled out his sheet from his folder, laid it out on Charles' desk and asked, "Can I show you something?"

"By all means. What have you got?"

"My life has been turned upside down in the last twenty four hours. Heck, in the last eight hours. And yet, I have met the most amazing people who have been here to support me. Total strangers, really. People who have followed their passion, tuned out negativity, and have pointed me toward a number of useful solutions and options. It seems that everything you've just said has corroborated the ideals these people live by," Ralph slid the piece of paper to Charles.

- PURSUE YOUR PASSION

- ENGAGE A TRUSTED BUSINESS ADVISOR, COACH, OR RESPECTED ALLY
- STAY AWAY FROM NEGATIVITY
- BE OPEN TO NEW DIRECTIONS
- RELATIONSHIPS / FAMILY MATTER
- YOUR IDENTITY IS MORE THAN JUST 'STUFF'
- KEEP A ROUTINE
- SWALLOW YOUR PRIDE

Charles was impressed. "You've obviously understood the essence of what you're going through and how to best cope through this difficult time." He jotted a few words at the bottom of the list before slithering the sheet back across the table.

Ralph accepted it into his hands and held it up to his face for analysis.

- NETWORK, NETWORK, NETWORK!
- HAVE FAITH—GOOD COMES FROM THIS

"I have to confess, I am not sure how the limited network that I've just met here will help me when I leave here. Or Rashida. Or any of the people I've met so far," Ralph pondered aloud.

"That's a fair statement. The answer lies in what is your ultimate goal? Some people cannot muster the courage and flexibility it takes to follow a new direction so they return to the same mentality that keeps them grounded in their previous circumstances. Others, knowing that this is an opportunity to do something more with their lives, embrace the change and go full throttle trying to use all available resources to them to get them into something better. So, let's focus on you. What is the change you need to make in order to get you to where you want to go?"

Ralph was stuck. He hadn't wanted or anticipated any changes before today. He was perfectly content doing exactly what he'd been doing. Well, sort of. Minus the marital separation. And the positional ambiguity at work. And the uncertainty of his future at PhasInt. And the deteriorating relationship with his son. And his lack of a social outlet or his growing waistline. Other than that, yeah, sure, everything was fine.

"I need to find a new job. I got fired today." There, he said it.

"Okay, let's talk about networking for a job. You will naturally reach out to those you know well, it's just human nature once the shock of termination wears off. You'll likely communicate with those already or still in a stable organization, most of whom have never experienced losing a job or being out of work. They will likely not know how to respond or react to you and your needs right now. When you've lived through this type of life experience, you get it and know the drill."

Ralph looked at him blankly.

"What I mean to say is that who you've relied on previously may not be a good fit for you now and it may be a painful realization that who you think are your closest network of your previous colleagues whom you've known for years won't be willing or able to help you. Yet, many new contacts and acquaintances will. It's counterintuitive — the ones who don't know you will help you but the ones who do won't. Once you realize who can help you, you can exert your time and energy to get to where you want to go."

"That doesn't make any sense to me. These new acquaintances you're talking about don't know me or my capabilities. Besides, where am I going to find these mysterious people who will want to help me? It's not like they are sitting around waiting to help Ralph Pibbs."

Ralph was dubious and a bit cynical. He'd never been out of a job before and was only acquainted with being one of the 'working ones'. In fact, whenever someone had left or gotten let go from PhasInt, Ralph never reached out to them after their departure. He figured he didn't need them in their new place of employment. Whether it was Joe from Sales or Mike from IT or Lauren from Marketing, he'd rarely given these folks another thought once they departed through the glass double doors. Even the man who hired him into PhasInt whom he had considered a mentor for the first few years of his career Ralph had not kept in contact with. Nor his last boss who left the company three years ago. Out of sight was definitely out of mind.

"I understand what you're saying but look at the people who have helped you today. You called them complete strangers. Fair enough. Now, let's look at your network from industry associations, executive groups, your alma mater's career resources, and even any social clubs you belong to and the role they can play in your search. Every group and individual with whom you come into contact is a great prospecting tool for your strategic networking. In fact, think of it as a safety net—a group who will be here to support you if you fall down. In this day and age where Department of Labor statistics indicate the average person will have had between 11-15 jobs in his career by the time he retires, there really can be nothing more important than one's network!" Charles was emphatic.

Ralph calculated that Mel alone had been fired by as many companies. He giggled to himself before Charles interrupted his silent thoughts. "Why don't you tell me about some of the extracurricular activities you've performed or undertaken in addition to your job?"

Ralph didn't have any. From working the ten to sixteen hour days, there was no time to have an external life. There was no time for family most days which is why Ralph moved into the city to be closer to work so he wouldn't lose so much time in the commute to the office. When was he supposed to make time in between the demands of his job to chitchat with people he didn't know and would lend no value to his current mission or position?

"I don't belong to any. It's all I could do to make my son's tee-ball and little league games," confessed Ralph.

"Then you need a fresh start. Make a list of all the organizations you could belong to like the FENG, the Executives Club, GPSEG, IERG, and others. These are industry or executive based groups who provide networking opportunities to like-minded individuals. Next you'll want to think about joining a coaching group like C12, Vistage or Gray Hair Management. I don't know if you qualify for YPO/WPO but that's another great organization…"

"Hold on. You're going too fast," Ralph cut Charles off for he was trying to capture each acronym and group onto the other side of his list of 10. He would need to research each of these groups and exactly how they could benefit Ralph as well as what Ralph could offer them.

Charles waited until Ralph stopped scribbling furiously, put his pen down and looked up again.

"Just to finish up on this, there are a lot of organizations out there designed to help you. You may also want to look at outplacement firms. There are a number of them and I suggest you get recommendations from others who have gone through their programs. Just know that they are devised to help you get to the heart of your existence, not necessarily get you a job. They want to get you in the RIGHT job. There's a big difference."

Ralph nodded his head while still scribbling. He looked over his notes and returned his eyes to meet Charles' stare.

"How is it that you know so much about this? Have you had a termination or layoff experience too?"

Charles folded his arms over his chest and shook his head. "No. I've been extremely fortunate throughout my career to not have had that unfortunate situation occur to me. But, I've seen it happen to plenty of friends, relatives and colleagues. I know it can be devastating."

Charles unfolded his hands and stood up. He pointed to one of the framed articles decorating the walls. "Do you see this article about me and the City Council? Or me with the Mayor? Or me with the State Representative? Here I am with the council of the top regional CEOs thanks to my involvement with a variety of associations, causes, and boards. I met those folks through the Leadership Philadelphia program, one of several leadership and networking programs that are offered throughout the country."

Charles paused long enough to gaze at Ralph before continuing.

"I'm thankful that I have chosen a number of activities to be involved with that have not pigeon-holed me but permitted me to fully leverage the breadth and scope of what I've learned and applied thus far in my career, which, in turn have been a boon to whichever organization I was with at the time."

Ralph wasn't sure if Charles was bragging about his own accomplishments or giving him personal examples and advice about the power of networking. "I don't see how you had the time to do all this if you had a day job too?"

"Like I said, it takes an extraordinary organization to see one's value and allow them to be free and do what they were meant to do. I excel in governance and social justice scenarios—I've fused the two together with my ability to network. I did a stellar job for whichever organization I was with at the time and was recognized as a subject matter expert in my field. So much so, that I decided to obtain a higher degree which gave me latitude to pursue a plethora of options. Boards sought me out, I spoke at conferences, and got involved in matters that meant the most to me. It is by no accident that I wound up overseeing the only house of its kind in the US that cares for thousands of people annually. My entire career has been formatted to seize opportunities that have been presented to me. All of them brought forward by multiple forms of networking," Charles sat back down.

"I'm too late to get started then. I should have been doing this years ago. Probably when I started my career?" Ralph lamented.

"It's never too late, Mr. Pibbs. May I call you Ralph? Ralph, look, now is not the time to give up hope! This is the perfect time to press the flesh, look someone in the eye, and demonstrate to them what value you can bring to an organization. You don't find jobs these days by trolling the internet. Even if you're an introvert, you can and must network! Call it humility, call it discomfort, call it whatever you want but you must get out to meet others. But first, you need to determine what it is you want to do. It's a perfect opportunity to change course, if you desire, and really see what it is that brings you joy. Look at this as a respite, an oasis in the middle of a desert," Charles was bubbling with enthusiasm.

"Hopefully this desert isn't as dry or as large as the Sahara!" Ralph was surprised to find himself making a funny, as his son would say when he thought something was amusing.

Have Faith: Something Good Comes From This

"The most important thing to remember is that this is not the end. This is a beginning. A new beginning. One where you can ask yourself new questions as to how you can increase not just your own paycheck but also your career and your life. What will be the value between you and your new organization? What do you want your legacy to be? Only when you have answered these questions to your satisfaction can you find a suitable match that aligns with your skills and values. I've seen all too often how many forego core values for the sake of a dollar—which is a value in and of itself. But, money can't buy you happiness. We see that every day in the lockers we have downstairs," Charles raised his eyebrows and cocked his head to point downward toward the chain link fenced area in the basement.

"True," Ralph agreed and followed Charles' eyebrows, recalling how most lockers downstairs were empty. Money did pay his mortgage, however, and values weren't earning him any cash right now. This was a lot for Ralph to process and his eyelids were feeling heavy from the events of the day and the many lessons bestowed.

"I can't stress the values part enough. Check out Glassdoor.com. Ask current and former employees about their experiences. You may have never anticipated to use these tools before but it will make such a difference to you in your transition. I am conscious of the fact that this may seem overwhelming to you. Daunting even. But, millions have gone through it and survived. And you will too. You are not alone in this and you will get through this. Just promise me one thing, Ralph," Charles halted his words for maximum effect.

"What's that?" inquired Ralph.

"Promise me that you won't go through this alone. Lean on your network whether your family, friends, colleagues or even any of us here at the House. There is always someone who can be your safety net and mark my words, you will see the good that comes out of this." Charles got up to indicate the conversation was over. He walked to the door and turned the handle to open it.

"I'm sure you could use a good night's sleep after what you've been through today," Charles declared.

"No truer words have been spoken, Charles. Thank you for your time and wisdom," responded Ralph who arose to meet Charles at the door.

Charles clasped Ralph's left shoulder with his massive right hand, gave him a squeeze, and said, "Have a good night."

"You too."

***

Ralph took a right out of Charles' office and found himself at the reception area in less than fifty steps. A new girl was at the desk reading a book. She didn't look up when Ralph approached. The foyer area was empty but he could hear a taped laugh track to a sitcom that was playing on the television in one of the guest lounges nearby. Ralph had no inclination to watch tv or mingle with the other residents. He was dog tired and ready to drift off into slumber-land.

He wondered how many people were in the house tonight? How many of them had lost all of their worldly possessions yet were now enjoying the gifts from altruistic strangers who only wanted to help a fellow human being? How many of the benefactors knew of the good they were contributing to on such a deeply profound and intimate level? Ralph turned his thoughts to the unemployed which now included amongst its ranks him.

How many people have been blindsided by the pronouncement of a termination? Did the companies contemplate their assessments or were they simply determined by economic forces? Personality? In Ralph's case, it seemed to be a combination of both as it could not have been for performance. At least no one had ever told him so.

Ralph had no opinion as to the emotions or situations of those at PhasInt who had been let go in the past. While there had never been an official or massive downsizing, there had been several restructurings within different departments. As none affected Ralph directly, he had no reason to meditate on the aftermath of those who left. Did they have families? What were their financial obligations? How soon thereafter were they able to find jobs? Were they treated with more dignity and respect than Ralph was afforded when he was escorted out of the building? What would people say about Ralph come Monday morning and he was no longer there? Would he be like the rest of the deposed: forgotten and ignored?

While Ralph convinced himself it would not matter what office gossip transpired on Monday, he knew his immediate challenge was what would occur tomorrow. Would his replacement credit cards arrive as promised? Would he have to wait until Monday because the shipping clerk missed the deadline to get them out today? Would his building manager call him back into the apartment immediately or would he have to spend the rest of the weekend in a hotel? When would he tell Connie and Michael the news of his termination and how would they take it? Would they treat him as coolly as his co-workers likely would? Could he count on their support like Charles insisted he should? Could he still be able to provide for his family even if they did not want his physical presence? Would he have to pass through this time alone, contrary to Charles' advice? Would he use this as a time to chart a new course starting with his first day as an independent? What would tomorrow bring?

The fear, uncertainty, and doubt swirled around in his mind trying to plant somewhere. Ralph fought the urge to let a negative foothold take root and attempted to recall from memory the ten truths he had learned in the past few hours.

The truths were comforting to him and he desperately wanted to believe in their validity and application to his current situation. Ralph knew he had failed at networking; he had never given it a thought previously. As Mel had insisted, just because he had failed at something did not mean he was a failure. Ralph wanted to hold on to this principle and the gift of newly-found humility.

He also wanted to make a plan for the coming days and weeks, although that would have to wait until tomorrow. Ralph didn't know if the computer room was still open but it didn't matter as he was inexorably drawn to his room. There were too many ideas, principles, concepts, and lists spinning around inside his brain.

He passed the reception and came to the elevator that had originally whisked him and LaShaun up to the second floor. He soon arrived at room 25, unlocked the door with the key from his pocket and stepped in. He latched the lock behind him and promptly entered the restroom to relieve himself and wash his hands.

He splashed water on his face, reached for the white, fluffy towel next to the sink, and cradled his head in his hands through the towel. He inhaled deliberately through the cloth and let out a pained sigh. Slowly lowering the towel to his chest, he gazed at himself in the mirror. He felt and looked defeated. Haggard. The man staring back at him was not the same one who, filled with promise, purpose and possibility, left to go to work this morning.

He put the towel neatly back on the rack and returned to staring at the foreigner before him. He abruptly left the bathroom and headed out the door of his room.

Humming 'na-na na, na-na na, na-na na na', Ralph hurriedly made his way back down the stairs to Charles' office, fingers clenching his sheet of paper with his list of ten. He hoped Charles hadn't left yet.

He rapped loudly on the door.

"Come in," was the reply.

Ralph swung the door open. "Would you mind if I made a personal call from your phone? I don't have any change to use the pay phone downstairs."

"By all means. I'll just step outside. Let me know when you're done," Charles responded. He looked to be in preparations for heading home judging by his hand on his briefcase, pushed the phone toward Ralph and said, "Just dial 9 to get an outside line."

"Thank you," Ralph mumbled.

His fingers trembled as he dialed the number. What if no one picked up? He wasn't sure what number would appear on the caller ID. He personally never picked up calls from unknown or foreign numbers.

He looked at his list one more time and drew a series of stars next to the fifth item. Charles advised him he couldn't do this alone.

- PURSUE YOUR PASSION
- ENGAGE A TRUSTED BUSINESS ADVISOR, COACH, OR RESPECTED ALLY
- STAY AWAY FROM NEGATIVITY
- BE OPEN TO NEW DIRECTIONS
- RELATIONSHIPS / FAMILY MATTER★★
- YOUR IDENTITY IS MORE THAN JUST 'STUFF'
- KEEP A ROUTINE
- SWALLOW YOUR PRIDE
- NETWORK, NETWORK, NETWORK!
- HAVE FAITH—GOOD COMES FROM THIS

The other end of the line rang. Once. Twice. On the third ring, a quizzical voice answered.

"Hello?"

"Hi baby. It's me. I'm coming home."

RESOURCES

APPENDIX A
EXECUTIVE NETWORKING ASSOCIATIONS

ACG—Association for Corporate Growth
www.acg.org

About
ACG is a global organization with 56 chapters and over 14,500 members. Doing business is at the heart of the ACG membership experience. Chapters in North and South America, Europe and Asia bring dealmakers together to help them achieve their business and professional goals.

Membership
Rates vary from $170 - $695 according to local chapter joined in the US. International rates vary for global chapters. Please apply online.

Contact Information
ACG Global Headquarters
125 S. Wacker Drive, Suite 3100
Chicago, IL 60606
Phone: (877) 358-2220 or (312) 957-4281
sforesman@acg.org

***

Belizean Grove
www.belizeangrove.org

About
The Belizean Grove is an international nurture network that helps women pursue more significant dreams, ambitions, purposes, transcendence, and spiritual fulfillment, while also opening up more leadership opportunities to these women of diverse backgrounds, talents, ages, and skills.

Membership
Is strictly by invitation only.

Contact Information
Additional information can be obtained by filling out a contact request on the website.

***

C-200
www.c200.org

About
The Committee of 200 is a membership organization of the world's most successful women entrepreneurs and corporate innovators. C200 has more than 400 members who collectively generate more than $1.4 trillion in annual revenues.

Membership
Members are nominated and evaluated against the following criteria:
Financial Responsibility
Leadership Qualities
Entrepreneurial Spirit
Extraordinary Career Accomplishments
Additional Considerations

Contact Information
The Committee of 200
980 N. Michigan Avenue, Suite 1575
Chicago, IL 60611
Phone: (312) 255-0296
info@c200.org

***

CEO Clubs International
http://ceoclubs.org/index.php

About

Comprised of chapters in the U.S., India, South Africa, Greece, and China, CEO Clubs International is a 35-year-old nonprofit, by-invitation-only membership association. Members must be CEOs of businesses which have above $2,000,000 in annual sales. Our average club member has $20,000,000 in annual sales.

Membership
Executive (Full) Members are entitled to attend all events in all Chapters, free of charge. Entrepreneurial Members can attend one PAC and one regional event annually free of charge. Associate Members receive e-mail notifications and invitations to all events and receive favorable discounts on a special package of member benefits. Entrepreneurial Membership is $250/year with a $100 initiation fee upon application.

Contact Information
CEO Clubs International
333 W. 86th Street #1207
New York, NY 10024
Phone: (212) 925-7911
jmancuso@ceoclubs.org

***

The Chicago Network

www.thechicagonetwork.org

About
The Chicago Network (TCN) is an organization of Chicago's most distinguished professional women.

Membership
Membership in the Network is by invitation only. Prospective candidates must be nominated by a TCN member and seconded by at least two other members. Candidates and their organizations must meet criteria specific to their positions and their industries. Membership is limited to women leaders in the top echelon of their professions by virtue of their position in the professional community and/or service in the public interest, and who have demonstrated a strong and personal commitment to TCN's purpose of empowering women.

Contact Information
211 East Ontario, Suite 1700
Chicago, IL 60611-3272
Phone: (312) 787-1990
kbensen@thechicagonetwork.org

***

The CIO Roundtable
www.cioroundtable.org

About
The CIO Roundtable of Western New York is the premier networking group for IT executives in Rochester, NY. It is an informal group of local Information Technology leaders from various industries, assembled to network, communicate and solve problems in a non-competitive, non-selling, confidential environment.

Membership
Please contact for more information.

Contact Information
Gary Letter, Director
CIO Roundtable of Western New York

P.O. Box 199
Spencerport, NY 14559

Phone: (585) 694-6112
Fax: (888) 668-7698
info@cioroundtable.org

***

CISO Executive Network

http://www.cisoexecnet.com/

About

CISO Executive Network is a peer-to-peer professional organization serving information security, IT risk management, privacy, and compliance executives from large enterprises, including corporations, healthcare systems, universities, and utilities.

Membership

Candidates from corporations in one of the following tiers:

$1B+ organizations
Membership reserved for the CISO or equivalent position
May invite or nominate direct reports to attend events
May invite or nominate Director level or above to attend events

$500M to $1B organizations
Membership reserved for the CISO or equivalent position
May invite or nominate direct reports to attend events

$250M to $500M organizations
Membership reserved for the CISO or equivalent position

Contact Information
info@cisoexecnet.com

***

Ellevate
www.elevatenetwork.com

About
Ellevate is the leading professional women's networking organization committed to the economic empowerment of women globally.

Membership
There are several levels of membership.
Power Circle: Senior Level Professionals, Successful Entrepreneurs, Forces of Nature $1000
Investor: Mid-Career Professionals, Entrepreneurs, Agents of Change $250
Visionary: Young Professionals Hitting Their Career Stride $100
Student: Current Graduate & Undergraduate Students: $25

Contact Information
Ellevate

261 Madison Avenue, 10th Floor
New York, NY 10016
Phone: (646) 517-1160
info@ellevatenetwork.com

***

Executives' Association of San Diego

http://www.execs-sd.org/

About

The Executives' Association of San Diego is a prestigious network of the area's top business leaders to promote, facilitate, and further the interchange of business information - enabling members to secure new business and increase revenue.

Membership

Membership is limited to one firm in each business or professional classification. A prospective member will be screened for possible conflicts and then invited to attend a meeting as a guest. There is a credit background check. Dues include a one-time initiation fee of $500 and monthly dues - $190.

Contact Information
Executives' Association of San Diego
302 Washington Street, #425
San Diego, CA 92103
Phone/FAX: (619) 255-4534
admin@execs-sd.org

***

The Executive Club
http://execclub.org

About

The Executive Club is a loosely organized group of those at the executive level in their careers that spans across all professional working industries.

Membership
Membership in The Executive Club is free.

Contact Information
Sean Rehder, Group Moderator
sean@execclub.org

***

EGG—Executive Girlfriends Group
http://executivegirlfriendsgroup.com

About
The Executive Girlfriends Group is a Women's Network, founded on National Girlfriends' Day in 2008 by Chicke Fitzgerald. The group hosts a weekly call, with interviews of authors and experts on a wide range of topics.

Membership
Charter corporate membership is $5,000 annually.
Individual membership $99 annually (fee waived if "between successes").

Contact Information
8710 W. Hillsborough Avenue Suite 315
Tampa, FL 33615
Phone: (813) 925-0789
egg@solutionz.com

***

ENGCHGO—Executive Network Group of Chicago

http://engchgo.org/
About

The Executive Network Group of Greater Chicago, Inc. (ENG) is organized under IRS Code as a Not-For-Profit Organization.

Membership
All ENG members have held titles such as, Manager, Director, Vice President, President, CFO, COO, CEO, and CIO with a minimum base salary level of $100,000. The annual membership fee is $100 per year.

Contact Information
Executive Network Group of Greater Chicago
3509 Surrey Lane
Long Grove, IL 60047
director@engchgo.org

***

The Executive Network of Seattle

www.tenseattle.org

About
The Executive Network of Seattle (TENS) is a vibrant community of business leaders who gather to support each other and learn about current and future business and socio-economic trends.

Membership
Dues range from $50-$240 per year.
Experience must include:
1. A minimum of 10 years direct management experience AND
2. A minimum of 2 years executive experience as a corporate officer/board member; entrepreneur/founder; senior corporate manager, director level/management consultant; or elected public official AND
3. Direct responsibility for executive functions including planning, organizing, staffing, directing and controlling an enterprise, and for annual budgets in the millions of dollars.

Contact Information

president@tenseattle.org

***

FENG--Financial Executives Networking Group
http://www.thefeng.org/

About

The Financial Executives Networking Group was founded as a forum for senior financial executives to share job opportunities and experiences. Members have held titles such as Chief Financial Officer, Controller, Treasurer, Managing Director, as well as Vice President of Tax, Mergers & Acquisitions, or Internal Audit.

Membership
Membership is free. In addition, you must have a sponsor.

Contact Information
MattBud@TheFENG.org
Phone: (203) 227-8965
Fax: (203) 227-8984

***

FEW—Forum of Executive Women
www.forumofexecutivewomen.com

About

The Forum of Executive Women is a membership organization of 350 women of significant influence across the Greater Philadelphia region. The Forum's membership is comprised of individuals holding the senior-most positions in the corporations, not-for-profit organizations and public sector entities that drive our regional economy and community.

Membership
Membership in the Forum of Executive Women is by invitation only.

Contact Information

1231 Highland Avenue
Fort Washington, PA 19034
Phone: (215) 628-9944
Fax: (215) 628-9839
Email: info@forumofexecutivewomen.com

***

The Global Leaders
www.tgleaders.com

About
We help our members to connect, share knowledge, information and insights, and build business and professional relationships. We have included in our site many very progressive web tools and features that we hope our members will find valuable. These include search features, education tools, funding tools, ranking systems, and tables, and the ability to post videos, documents and your own stores.

Membership
Executive Premium Plan ($25/month) allows full use of all services and features. This includes creating groups, commenting on groups, discussions, and connections, including file downloading privileges. Basis membership is free and allows access to the networks and key site features. Does not give access to detailed membership databases.

Contact Information
Please sign up via our website.
http://www.linkedin.com/in/bickerstaff
gbickerstaff@tgleaders.com

***

GPSEG—Greater Philadelphia Senior Executive Group
http://gpseg.org

About
GPSEG is a non-profit professional association of senior-level executives committed to the exchange of business contacts and ideas in a spirit of generous giving, and to the fostering of career

fulfillment, business development, and professional and personal growth.

Membership
Membership in GPSEG is by invitation only and has very stringent membership requirements including being a "C" level executive (or equivalent); compensation level of $150k or more of base compensation before bonus for public and private industry; in the not-for-profit sectors, we consider "C" level compensation to be approximately $100k; “C” level should generally include about 20 years of experience or a lesser period of time for extraordinary career advancement and achievement.

Contact Information
Maureen Waddington, Administrator
Phone: (215) 393-3144
Fax: (215) 893-4872
maureen.waddington@comcast.net
P.O. Box 187, Montgomeryville, PA 18936
Assistant: Linda Volmis, lvolmis@comcast.net

***

Hartford/Springfield Executive Roundtable Network

http://www.linkedin.com/groups?gid=1678907&trk=group-name

About
This group was formed by and for those in the Hartford metro area that have in the past or currently are in senior executive roles who recognize the power of “pay it forward” networking and willing to give more than they receive by joining the group.

Membership
Past or current career requirements include reporting within 1 level from the CEO; up to 4 levels in Fortune 500 organizations; at least 7 years of managerial responsibility; responsibility for at least 10 subordinate employees (not all direct reports); annual revenue

responsibility or operating budget of at least $10 million; and executive-level compensation of at least $125,000.

Contact Information
Phone: (918) 938-1398
DavidK05@msn.com
http://www.linkedin.com/in/davidkrysh

***

IERG—International Executives Resource Group
www.iergonline.org

About
The International Executive Resources Group is a source of global contacts, referrals, and knowledge pools - a network of field-tested advice and counsel from experienced peers.

Membership
Members must meet strict criteria including living and working outside one's home country for a minimum of three + years; significant senior executive level background (e.g. C-Level or reporting to C-Level functions in a corporate setting or its equivalent) with considerable experience in leading other executives; has earned a minimum annual base salary of the equivalent of USD $200,000. Dues are $150 per year

Contact Information
3 Anchorage Way
Old Saybrook, CT 06475
Phone: (860) 984-6186
Fax: (860) 510-0249
rbardos@iergonline.org

***

IWF—International Women's Forum

www.iwforum.org

About

The International Women's Forum advances leadership across careers, cultures and continents by connecting the world's most preeminent women of significant and diverse achievement.

Membership

Membership in the International Women's Forum (IWF) is by invitation and is influenced by definitive international standards.

Contact Information
2120 L Street, NW
Suite 460
Washington, DC 20037
Phone: (202) 387-1010
Fax: (202) 387-1009
iwf@iwforum.org

***

MAENG—Madison Area Executive Networking Group
http://www.linkedin.com/groups?gid=1866628&trk=group-name
About
MAENG holds structured networking meetings for professionals/execs in $100K+ to revitalize job search efforts.

Membership
Please contact us on LinkedIn for membership information

Contact Information
49 Kessel Court, Ste. 103, Madison, WI 53711
Phone: (608) 274-2430
Clara.Nydam@CareerMomentum.com

***

McDermott & Bull Executive Network
www.mbexec.net

About
McDermott & Bull Executive Network is dedicated to providing valuable resources for senior level executives and creating opportunities to build networking relationships, both in person and within our online community.

Membership
Please apply online.

Contact Information
2 Venture, Suite 100
Irvine, CA 92618
Phone: (949) 753-1700

***

MENG—Marketing Executive Networking Group
www.mengonline.com

About
MENG is a national network of top-level marketing executives devoted to enhancing its members' professional skills, relationships, and knowledge and prides itself on a culture of genuine camaraderie.

Membership
MENG members are Marketing, Sales, or General Management executives whose primary focus is, or was at one time in their career, marketing whose minimum base salary is $160,000 and has held the title of Vice-President, or equivalent, and above.

Contact Information
Joey Iazzetto, Chairman of MENG
Must apply online

***

NACD—National Association of Corporate Directors

www.nacdonline.org

About

NACD's mission is to advance exemplary board leadership -for directors, by directors by delivering the knowledge and insight that board members need to confidently navigate complex business challenges and enhance shareowner value.

Membership
To qualify for NACD membership, you must be an active director on the board of a public, private or nonprofit organization, or a senior-level executive serving on the board of an organization enrolling in NACD Full Board Membership.

Contact Information
2001 Pennsylvania Ave, NW, Suite 500
Washington, DC 20006
Phone: (202) 775-0509
Fax: (202) 775-4857
kkdodd@nacdonline.org

***

North Canton Executive Networking Group
_http://www.linkedin.com/groups?gid=2319089&trk=hb_side_g

About
The North Canton Executive Networking Group is a Northeast Ohio networking group dedicated to helping professionals find jobs by providing best-practice guidance, networking opportunities and support.

Membership
This is a free networking and support group for those executives in Northeast Ohio who are unemployed, underemployed or seeking to network.

Contact Information
Please contact us on LinkedIn

***

PSPS—Philadelphia Society of People & Strategy
www.peopleandstrategy.org

About
The Philadelphia Society of People & Strategy is the premier organization for exchanging ideas and knowledge among the Greater Philadelphia Region's HR and business leaders.

Membership

Individual membership is $225 annually. Those in transition receive complimentary membership for 6 months. Applications and membership criteria can be found online.

Contact Information
Philadelphia Society of People & Strategy
P.O. Box 1155, Havertown, PA 19083
Phone: (800) 871-9012 x78777
Info@peopleandstrategy.org

***

SENG - Senior Executive Networking Group - New England

www.seng-ne.org

About
The Senior Executive Networking Group of New England is an opportunity for seasoned executives from all business functional areas to meet on a regular basis.

Membership

Because SENG-NE is an invitation-only organization, interested parties cannot apply for membership. If you are interested in joining SENG-NE, you must be invited by an existing member. Dues are $50.

Contact Information

admin@seng-ne.org

***

SIM—Society for Information Management

www.simnet.org

About
SIM is an association of senior IT executives, prominent academicians, selected consultants, and other IT thought leaders built on the foundation of local chapters, who come together to share and enhance their rich intellectual capital for the benefit of its members and their organizations.

Membership
SIM's member categories are:
* Practitioner--A senior-level IT professional in either a public or private sector organization meeting the following criteria:
* Corporate/divisional head of a corporate or divisional IS organization.
* Member of an IS management staff supporting corporate/divisional IS heads with key management roles, as certified by the head of the organization.
* Academic--A full-time university or college faculty member making a significant contribution to the IS field. *
Consultant--Leaders at the partner/principal level who influence the direction of their own company or their clients' companies, and who directly contribute to the IS profession.

Membership costs range from individual level ($80-285) to corporate ($420-$27,500)

Contact Information
Society for Information Management
15000 Commerce Parkway, Suite C
Mount Laurel, NJ 08054
Phone: (800) 387-9746
Fax: (856) 439-0525
sim@simnet.org

***

Tech Execs Network

www.techexecs.net

About

The TechExecs Network™ (www.TechExecs.Net) continues to advance the careers of the next generation of IT Leadership, promote stability, connections, and advocacy for the Information Technology community as a whole, and provide an interactive forum for over 370,000 contacts nation-wide.

Membership
Industry: $199 fees are reserved for IT professionals at all levels.
Solution: $1500 fees are reserved for solution providers and firms that service the technology industry which are not Industry level memberships.
Affiliate: $49 fees are semi-annual memberships for those in transition and students.

Contact Information
TechExecs Network
14090 SW Freeway, Suite 300-189
Sugar Land, Texas 77478
Phone: (866) 661-0258
Fax: (832) 201-9423

***

TENG—Technology Executives Networking Group
http://theteng.org

About

The TENG is dedicated to empowering technology executives to enhance their careers through networking.

Membership

TENG members are current and former Chief Information Officers, Chief Technology Officers, Senior Vice Presidents, Vice Presidents, and Directors of technology.

Membership is free of charge.

Contact Information
Technology Executives Networking Group
Edward J. Pospesil & Company
221 Driftwood Lane, Guilford, CT 06437-1922
Phone: (203) 458-6566
Fax: (203) 458-6564
ed@ejp.com

***

Washington Network Group
http://www.washingtonnetworkgroup.com

About
The Washington Network Group (WNG) is a membership organization of professionals in business, finance, technology, foreign and government affairs.

Membership
Members may access our password-protected Member Directory online. Members and non-members may join our LinkedIn groups, our Facebook group, and follow us on Twitter.
Membership is by application, and annual dues are $90.

Contact Information
Washington Network Group
Post Office Box 571
McLean, Virginia 22101
Phone: (202) 455-4504
admin@washingtonnetworkgroup.com

***

WCD—Women Corporate Directors

www.womencorporatedirectors.com

About
WCD is the only global membership organization and community of women corporate directors.

Membership
Members serve as directors of both Global Stock Exchanges. WCD Members are usually very senior, influential executives (Chairmen, CEO's, COO's and other C-level executives). Apply online.

Contact Information

Susan Stautberg, CEO, Co-Founder, and Global Co-Chair, Henrietta Fore, Global Co-Chair and Alison Winter, Co-Founder
info@womencorporatedirectors.com

***

APPENDIX B

EXECUTIVE COACHING GROUPS

The Brain Trust
www.braintrustceo.com

About
The Brain Trust, based in Atlanta, GA, is a fifteen year old organization of CEOs, company presidents, general managers and business owners who come together during a monthly CEO conference to provide insight and solutions to shared business hurdles through half day meetings.

Membership
To become a member of our CEO conference, you must be one of the following: CEO, President, Business Owner, General Manager, Managing Partner of a Company

Contact Information
Tom Cramer, Co-Chairman
1010 Olde Towne Lane
Woodstock, GA 20189
Phone: (770) 924-2883
tcramer@braintrustceo.com

***

Bridgestar
www.bridgestar.org

About
Bridgestar (www.bridgestar.org) provides a nonprofit management job board, content, and tools designed to help nonprofit organizations build strong leadership teams and individuals pursue career paths as nonprofit leaders.

Membership
To join one of our groups on LinkedIn please join LinkedIn (free) and ensure your profile is up to date.

Contact Information
Jeff Bradach Managing Partner and Co-Founder
Bridgestar c/o The Bridgespan Group
535 Boylston Street,
10th Floor
Boston, MA 02116
Phone: (617) 572-2833
bridgestar@bridgespan.org

***

C12 Group
www.c12group.com

About
More than just a Christian CEO roundtable, C12 members minister to each other via transparent discussion and prayer.

Membership
Minimum Qualifications: Christian business leaders (CEOs, Owners, or Presidents) with responsibility for five or more employees. Generally, those running businesses with ten or more employees are able to delegate and arrange their schedule to permit regular monthly attendance without interrupting business.
Cost: C12 offers tiered pricing based on company size to ensure affordability without compromising excellence/quality.

Contact Information
Buck Jacobs, Founder and Chairman
Don Barefoot, President and CEO
The C12 Group, LLC.
4101 Piedmont Parkway
Greensboro, NC 27410
Phone: (336) 841-7100

***

Career Place
www.mycareerplace.org

About
We teach successful job search skills and firmly and compassionately coach you for the length of the job search. Our services will put you on the right path and give you the discipline, skills and stamina to find your next great job.

Membership
For a $150 annual fee, our members have access to a complete portfolio of job search services, packaged in a best in class job search training curriculum. Unlimited access to our workshops, coaches, Career Corner program, and computer and office support are included in membership.

Contact Information
600 Hart Road, Suite 118
Barrington, IL 60010
Phone: (847) 304-4157
Info@mycareerplace.org

***

CEN—Chief Executive Network
SEN—Senior Executive Network

https://www.chiefexecutivenetwork.com/default.aspx

About
The goal of Chief Executive Network (CEN) and Senior Executive Network (SEN) is to improve your company's performance by working "on" your business as opposed to "in" your business. Our meetings allow for this through networking and the exchange of expertise with your peers.

Membership
Prospective members may complete the application and e-mail, cen@chiefexec.com, or fax, 785-832-0404. There is a onetime prospective member application fee of $950 USD. The application fee includes the application process and attendance at your first

meeting. You must attend an initial meeting and be asked to join the membership. After your first meeting and membership approval, there is an annual (or bi-annual) fee for membership determined by your company's gross revenue from the previous fiscal year.

Contact Information
Bob Grabill, President and CEO
Phone: (785) 832-0303 x 102
bgrabill@chiefexec.com

***

CEO Connection
www.ceoconnection.com

About
CEO Connection is the only membership organization in the world reserved exclusively for CEOs of mid-market companies—companies with between $100 million and $3 billion in annual revenue. Through in-person events, specialized online and offline communications, and personal, individualized attention, we connect thousands of mid-market CEOs to the people, information and resources that can make them more successful.

Membership
Prospective members must meet one of the following titles: CEO, Chairman of the Board, President, Managing Director, General Manager, Managing Partner, COO, Executive Director, Publisher AND meeting all of the following criteria:

- Must run a company, division, or unit with annual revenues $100M -- $3Bn
- Receive a nomination from an existing CEO Connection member or strategic partner
- Show leadership in his/her respective field and in social endeavors
- Demonstrate personal and professional integrity
- Be willing and able to help other CEOs succeed

Membership rates range between $6000 -- $30,000

Contact Information
Membership@ceoconnection.com

***

The CEO Forum
http://www.theceoforum.us/

About
With the ideas of others and the knowledge you will gain, both your key people and your company will benefit. All forums are recorded, so if an executive happen to miss one, it is available to members, CEOs and your staff.

Membership
From this diverse group of CEOs, you will learn a lot. Our regular Forums average over 150 years of experience. You'll learn things that can help you now and in the future at no cost to you.

Contact Information
wcf@theceoforum.us

***

Chief Financial Officer Forum
http://www.thecfo-forum.com/

About
The CFO Forum will provide you with key strategies to stay competitive at time when it is most critical for CFOs to stay ahead of the curve. With the role of the CFO continuing to grow and change, it is imperative to get the latest information as it relates to this evolving executive position.

Membership
Attendance as a delegate is free of charge, but by personal invitation only.
Contact Information
Shelton Hollers

Project Manager
shollers@richmondevents.com
Phone: (212) 651-8700
Fax: (212) 651-8701
general@richmondevents.com

***

Chief Operating Officer Forum
http://cooforum.org/

About
COO Forum's Mission is professional development for Second-in-Command Executives through peer-to-peer collaboration, education, forums, networks, employing a local, regional, national, and global approach.

Membership
The COO Forum is open to all business leaders who are responsible for the operations of their company or division. Dues are $750.00 Annually or $75.00 Monthly

Contact Information
Executive Director, Bill Shepard
bshepard@COOForum.org
Chief Operating Officer Business Forum, Inc.
14435 Big Basin Way, Suite # 210
Saratoga, CA 95070
Phone: (408) 292-1593
Fax: (408) 521-2180

***

Clear Circles

www.lasallenonprofitcenter.org/pdf/clearcircles/guidestar_article.pd
f
About

With a focus on non-profit leadership, Clear Circles focuses on group members helping each other achieve their professional and even personal goals through highly focused questioning and the exchange of feedback. At the end of each session, participants reflect on the quality of the process to ensure that it remains highly relevant and productive.

Membership
Each participant pays $380 for all nine sessions, if they have a membership in the Nonprofit Center. The cost for non-members is $450.

Contact Information
Sonia Stamm, Director of Leadership Initiatives at the Nonprofit Center
Phone: (215) 951-1711
stamm@lasalle.edu

***

<u>The Commonwealth Institute</u>
www.commonwealthinstitute.org

About
The Commonwealth Institute (TCI) is a vibrant, nonprofit organization founded to help women business become and stay successful.

Membership
Our membership includes CEOs, senior corporate executives, directors of nonprofits and proven solo professionals – women who are committed to working on their respective businesses. Membership is $395/year; Affiliate membership is $295/year and Forum membership is $1500-3500/year. Please apply online.

Contact Information
101 Federal Street, Suite 1900
Boston, MA 02110
(617) 342-7172

or
16850-112 Collins Avenue
Sunny Isles Beach, FL 33160
(305) 799-6547
kdoyle@commonwealthinstitute.org
mkirchheimer@commonwealthinstitute.org

***

The Entrepreneur Organization Network
www.eonetwork.org

About

The Entrepreneurs' Organization (EO) is a global business network of 9,500+ business owners in 131 chapters and 40 countries who educate, transform, inspire and offer invaluable resources in the form of events, leadership-development programs, an online entrepreneur forum, and business owner education opportunities, among other resources designed for business growth.

Membership
You must first apply to their local chapter, where local leadership will ensure you meet the EO membership criteria.
Members pay both chapter and Global dues in one annual membership payment. Global dues are currently US$1,700, plus a one-time US$800 initiation fee, and are prorated based on the fiscal month you join.

Contact Information
500 Montgomery Street, Suite 700
Alexandria, VA 22314 USA
Phone: (703) 519-6700
Fax: (703) 519-1864
Info@eonetwork.org

***

Executives Network

www.executivesnetwork.com

About

Executives Network is focused on one thing – helping executives land their next position. Gone are the days of someone tapping you on the shoulder for the next opportunity. These days, you actually have to be extremely prepared, proactive and targeted. Executives Network helps you with that process. We have in-person meetings in select cities throughout the U.S. For people outside those cities, we have solid networks throughout the country to aid in the job search.

Membership

Premium Members enjoy a number of benefits including access to a national peer network of other executives who want to help you in your job search, a library of webinars with innovative tips and techniques to help reduce the time it takes to land the next job, and custom LinkedIn Reviews (for annual and semi-annual members) where we'll go through your LinkedIn profile and ensure you're attracting the right people to your profile.

Membership is available on a monthly, quarterly, semiannual or annual basis. Many members remain active after landing their dream job in order to help others and to keep their options open going forward.

Contact Information

en@executivesnetwork.com

***

<u>G100 Network</u>
www.G100Network.com

About

G100 Network is a group of private learning communities for current and rising CEOs and the most senior executives who work with them. G100 Network consists of:

* G100, a private group of chief executives of the world's largest and most significant companies. CEO members gather twice each year for off-the-record, candid conversations about leadership, strategy, and navigating the current business environment.

* G100 Next Generation Leadership, a one-year intensive and transformative program that develops the future generation of executive leaders. Participants – senior level officers, including CEO succession candidates – share the room with CEOs and other seasoned practitioners to learn how to address tomorrow's business challenges.

* G100 Talent Consortium, a network of CEOs, CHROs, and other talent executives focused on leveraging human capital to drive business results. Members gather twice each year for private conversations to create forward-looking talent strategies and exchange ideas that members can act on the next day.

Membership
Please contact G100 directly for membership criteria.

Contact Information

Courtney Komar

G100 Network

630 Fifth Avenue, Suite 3210New York NY 10111

Phone: (212) 332-6324

G100@G100.com

***

Genius Network
www.geniusnetwork.com

About
Genius Network® Is An Ever Expanding System Of Increasing Cooperation And Creativity Among Unique Ability Achievers. Your Ultimate Resource To Creating An ELF™ (Easy, Lucrative, & Fun) Business.

Membership
Genius Network® Members gain confidence and direction in their lives and businesses. This is not your typical brainstorm group; you will not experience anything like this anywhere else. Visit www.GeniusNetwork.com and find out if you qualify. Dues: $25,000.

Contact Information
Joe Polish

Pirahna Marketing Inc.

4440 S. Rural Rd., Bldg. F

Tempe, AZ 85282, USA

Phone: (480) 858-0008

Fax: (480) 858-0004

Eunice@joepolish.com

***

Gray Hair Management
www.grayhairmanagement.com

About
The Gray Hair Management corporate mission is to help professionals get jobs. All of our activities are focused on this mission, whether it is to help organizations and recruiters find qualified candidates, provide our members with networking events

and job leads, or to help individuals secure their next position with our exclusive Pathways Through Transition Coaching program.

Membership
Quarterly membership fee $24.00

Contact Information
Gray Hair Management, LLC
1450 American Lane
Suite 1400
Schaumburg, IL 60173
Phone: (847) 940-2800 or (877) 975-2800

***

Kelleher Associates
http://www.kelleherllc.com/

About
Kelleher Associates is the Philadelphia region's premier career transition and executive coaching firm.

Membership

- Association for Corporate Growth
- Business Leaders Network
- Forum of Executive Women
- Greater Philadelphia Chamber of Commerce
- Greater Philadelphia Senior Executive Group
- Mid-Atlantic Capital Alliance
- Main Line Chamber of Commerce
- Mid-Atlantic Employers' Association
- Philadelphia HR Planning Society
- ExecuNet
- AIPAC
- Board Source
- Pennsylvania BIO
- PA Direct Marketing Association
- PACT

Contact Information

Four Glenhardie Corporate Center
1255 Drummers Lane, Suite 103
Wayne, PA 19087-1565
Phone: (610) 293-1115
Fax: (610) 293-1116
mcarter@kelleherllc.com

***

Savor the Success (6 Figure and 7 Figure Women)
http://www.savorthesuccess.com/

About
Our mission is to maximize the strengths of each client in transition, executives contemplating a career change, and high potential men and women identified as critical talent within their organization.

Membership
The 7-Figure Club By Invitation Only
The 6-Figure Club $495 / Month
In-Person Premium Membership $79 / Month
Online Premium Membership $49 / Month

Contact Information
Angela Jia Kim and Marc Stedman Co-Founders of Savor the Success
info@savorthesuccess.com

***

Vistage
www.vistage.com

About
Vistage International has global affiliates in 16 countries. Our Executive Leadership Program members meet in small peer advisory groups every month under the same guiding principles—to help one another become better leaders, make better decisions and achieve better results.

Membership
Vistage has more than 16,000 members, largely CEOs and business owners, from 15 countries who attend monthly peer group meetings. Fees range between $8,000-$16,000/year.

Contact Information
Vistage International
World Headquarters
11452 El Camino Real
Suite 400
San Diego, CA 92130
Phone: (858) 523-6800 or (800) 589-0531
Fax: (858) 523-6802

***

<u>Women President's Organization</u>

www.womenpresidents.org

About
The WPO is a non-profit membership organization for women presidents of multimillion-dollar companies. The members of the WPO take part in professionally-facilitated peer advisory groups in order to bring the 'genius out of the group' and accelerate the growth of their businesses.

Membership

Fees range between $1800 – $5000 per year, be certified a woman owned business and have a woman as majority owner.

Contact Information
155 E. 55th Street
Suite 4H
New York, NY 10022
Phone: (212) 688-4114
Fax: (212) 688-4766

Marsha Firestone, PhD—President and Founder
marsha@womenpresidentsorg.com

***

World50
www.world50.com

About
World50 is a private community for senior-most executives from globally respected organizations to intimately share ideas, solutions and collaborative discovery free from press, competition and solicitation.

Membership
Is strictly by invitation only.

Contact Information
Phone: (404) 816-5559
inquiries@world50.com

***

World Presidents Organization/Young Presidents Organization
http://www.wpo.org
About
WPO provides YPO graduates with opportunities for continued learning and lifelong peer networking at the chapter, regional and international levels.

Membership
You are eligible to join WPO if you graduated from YPO or if you left YPO in good standing and were a member for at least three years (excluding any grace period).

Contact Information
YPO-WPO
600 East Las Colinas Boulevard, Suite 1000
Irving, TX 75039

Phone: (800) 773-7976 or (972) 587-1500
Fax: (972) 587-1600
info@wpo.org

***

APPENDIX C

EXECUTIVE OUTPLACEMENT FIRMS

6 Figure Jobs
https://www.6figurejobs.com/

About
6FigureJobs is tailored for executives & senior-level professionals only. Our members and clients connect faster than they do through larger career sites

Membership
FREE Basic Membership

Contact Information
Chris Miller, Principal
397 Post Rd Apt 201
Darien, CT 06820-3645,
United States
Phone: (203) 655-0649
Fax: (203) 656-9595

***

Blue Steps
https://www.bluesteps.com/Home.aspx

About

BlueSteps is an online career management service for senior executives. As an exclusive service of the Association of Executive Search Consultants (AESC), BlueSteps enables senior executives to be visible to more than 8,000 AESC member executive search professionals who use BlueSteps to locate candidates. BlueSteps also offers a full suite of career management tools and resources specifically for senior-level executives.

Membership

A one time fee of $298 (or regional equivalent) will apply. Certain premium services will require annual renewal.

Contact Information
Phone: (800) 363-1207
info@bluesteps.com

***

Career Partners International
www.cpiworld.com

About
Career Partners International has grown to be the world's largest and most successful talent management consultancy. Headquartered in Chapel Hill, North Carolina, Career Partners International has more than 250 offices in over 45 countries around the world, and offers direct access to more than 1600 experts in career management, talent development, leadership and executive coaching, career transition and outplacement services.

Contact Information
Please fill out our online form at our website www.cpiworld.com.
Phone: (800) 686-5999 or (919) 401-4273

***

Challenger, Gray, and Christmas
http://www.challengergray.com/

About
Challenger, Gray & Christmas, Inc. is the nation's first, oldest and premier outplacement consulting organization.

Membership
In order to enter one of our outplacement programs, we require sponsorship by an employee's company.

Contact Information

John Challenger, CEO
150 S. Wacker Dr., Ste. 2700
Chicago, IL 60606,
Phone: (312) 332-5790
Fax: (312) 332-4843
info@challengergray.com

***

<u>ExecuNet</u>

http://execunet.com/

About
ExecuNet has over 20 years experience helping top-flight executives succeed in their careers and business. ExecuNet is a private business network with continuing benefits for senior-level executives.

Membership
30-Day Option $39. Membership automatically renews every 30 days at the rate of $39.
90-Day Option $99. At the end of 90 days, membership automatically renews every 30 days at the rate of $39.
180-Day Option $219. Our most popular membership according to executives surveyed in ExecuNet's Executive Job Market Intelligence Report, the average executive expects to be in job search at least 6 months.
360-Day Option $399

Contact Information
David Opton, CEO
295 Westport Ave.
Norwalk, CT 06851,
United States
Phone: (203) 750-1030
Toll Free: (800) 637-3126
Fax: (203) 840-8320

***

Executives Network
www.executivesnetwork.com

About
Executives Network is focused on one thing – helping executives land their next position. Gone are the days of someone tapping you on the shoulder for the next opportunity. These days, you actually have to be extremely prepared, proactive and targeted. Executives Network helps you with that process. We have in-person meetings in select cities throughout the U.S. For people outside those cities, we have solid networks throughout the country to aid in the job search.

Membership
Premium Members enjoy access to a national peer database with contact information, job search criteria and experience for all *Executives Network* members. They may also participate in affiliate programs and area-specific workshops and forums. Fees are either monthly ($39) or quarterly ($109), semiannually ($199) or annually ($379). Many members remain active after landing their dream job in order to help others and to keep their options open going forward.

Contact Information
Phone: (720) 981-3570
info@executivesnetwork.com

***

Ivy Executive
https://www.ivyexec.com/

About
Ivy Exec offers targeted resources that will shorten the job search timeline.

Contact Information
Elena Bajic

6 E 39th St Fl 11
New York, NY 10016-0112,
United States
Phone: (212) 431-3969

***

Lee Hecht Harrison
http://www.lhh.com/Pages/default.aspx

About
Lee Hecht Harrison is a talent solutions company focused on delivering Career Transition, Leadership Development, Career Development and Change Management solutions for organizations committed to developing their best talent and becoming employers of choice.

Contact Information
Peter Alcide, President and Chief Operating Officer
800.611.4544
50 Tice Blvd.
Woodcliff Lake, NJ 07677,
United States
Phone: (201) 930-9333
Fax: (201) 307-0878

***

Prositions

http://www.prositions.com/

About
Prositions was founded by a group of employees who were "downsized" after a corporate acquisition who decided to pool resources to provide outplacement help for the other employees who were let go.

Contact Information

Prositions, Inc.
6200 Aurora Avenue, Suite 410W
Urbandale, Iowa 50322
Toll free: (877) 244-8848
Tel: (515) 864-7200
Fax: (515) 309-4164
sales@prositions.com

***

Right Management
http://www.right.com/

About

Right Management is a global leader in talent and career management workforce solutions within Manpower Group. The firm designs and delivers solutions to align talent strategy with business strategy.

Contact Information
Douglas Matthews, President & COO
1818 Market Street, 33rd Fl.
Philadelphia, PA 19103-3614
United States
Phone: (215) 988-1588
Fax: (215) 988-0150

***

Stybel, Peabody & Associates
http://www.stybelpeabody.com/outplac.htm

About
Founded thirty years ago, Stybel Peabody & Associates, Inc., a Lincolnshire International Company, specializes in "smooth leadership change."

Contact Information

Maryanne Peabody, Co-founder
Stybel, Peabody & Associates

60 State Street, Suite 700

Boston, MA 02109
Tel. (617) 371-2990
peabody@stybelpeabody.com

***

ABOUT THE AUTHOR

Suzanne Garber has been featured in the NY Times, USA Today, US News & World Report, and BusinessWeek, amongst others, and has spoken at dozens of international association conferences focusing on risk mitigation, disaster recovery, medical and security networks, and globalization. Suzanne serves on the boards of several for profit, humanitarian and association organizations, including some listed in this book. A dual US-EU citizen who has lived in 8 countries on 4 continents and traveled to 80 nations, Suzanne holds a master's degree with honors from the University of Pennsylvania and a BA with honors in foreign languages from Rutgers University. A two-time cancer survivor, Suzanne splits her time between Philadelphia and Miami with her husband, Christopher, a disabled US Army veteran and champion martial artist, who is a saint to put up with her global wanderings. Suzanne invites you to connect with her on social media.

Columbia, SC
25 October 2018